Pass **ECDL4**

Module 7: Information and Communication

Using Internet Explorer 6 & Outlook Express 6

O.H.U. Heathcote

Published by

PAYNE-GALLWAY
PUBLISHERS LTD

26-28 Northgate Street, Ipswich IP1 3DB
Tel: 01473 251097 Fax: 01473 232758

www.payne-gallway.co.uk

Acknowledgements

Every effort has been made to contact copyright owners of material published in this book. We would be glad to hear from unacknowledged sources at the earliest opportunity.

Cover design by Direction Advertising and Design Ltd

First Edition 2004

A catalogue entry for this book is available from the British Library.

ISBN 1 904467 35 0

Copyright © O. H. U. Heathcote 2004

The ECDL Trade Mark is the registered trade mark of The European Computer Driving Licence Foundation Limited in Ireland and other countries.

This ECDL Foundation approved courseware product incorporates learning reinforcement exercises. These exercises are included to help the candidate in their training for the ECDL. The exercises included in this courseware product are not ECDL certification tests and should not be construed in any way as ECDL certification tests. For information about Authorised ECDL Test Centres in different National Territories please refer to the ECDL Foundation web site at www.ecdl.com

All rights reserved

Printed in Malta by Gutenberg Press

Disclaimer

"European Computer Driving Licence" and ECDL and Stars device are registered trade marks of The European Computer Driving Licence Foundation Limited in Ireland and other countries. Payne-Gallway Publishers is an independent entity from The European Computer Driving Licence Foundation Limited, and not affiliated with The European Computer Driving Licence Foundation Limited in any manner. Pass ECDL4 Module 7 may be used in assisting students to prepare for the ECDL Module 7 examination. Neither The European Computer Driving Licence Foundation Limited nor Payne-Gallway Publishers warrants that the use of this book (Pass ECDL4 Module 7) will ensure passing the ECDL Module 7 examination. Use of the ECDL-F Approved Courseware Logo on this product signifies that it has been independently reviewed and approved by ECDL-F as complying with the following standards:

Acceptable coverage of all courseware content related to the ECDL Version 4.0.

This courseware material has not been reviewed for technical accuracy and does not guarantee that the end user will pass the ECDL Module 7 examination. Any and all assessment items and/or performance based exercises contained in this book (Pass ECDL4 Module 7) relate solely to this book and do not constitute or imply certification by The European Driving Licence Foundation in respect of any ECDL examination. For details on sitting ECDL examinations in your country please contact your country's National ECDL/ICDL designated Licensee or visit The European Computer Driving Licence Foundation Limited web site at http://www.ecdl.com.

Candidates using this courseware material should have a valid ECDL/ICDL Skills Card. Without such a Skills Card, no ECDL/ICDL Examinations can be taken and no ECDL/ICDL certificate, nor any other form of recognition, can be given to the candidate.

ECDL/ICDL Skills Cards may be obtained from any Approved ECDL/ICDL Test Centre or from your country's National ECDL/ICDL designated Licensee.

References to the European Computer Driving Licence (ECDL) include the International Computer Driving Licence (ICDL). Version 4.0 is published as the official syllabus for use within the European Computer Driving Licence (ECDL) and International Computer Driving Licence (ICDL) certification programme.

Preface

Who is this book for?

This book is suitable for anyone studying for ECDL Version 4.0 (Module 7), either at school, adult class or at home. It is suitable for complete beginners or those with some prior experience, and takes the learner step-by-step from the very basics to the point where they will feel confident using the Internet and sending and receiving e-mails.

The approach

The approach is very much one of "learning by doing". The module is divided into a number of chapters which correspond to one lesson. The student is guided step-by-step through a practical task at the computer, with numerous screenshots to show exactly what should be on their screen at each stage. Each individual in a class can proceed at their own pace, with little or no help from a teacher. At the end of most chapters there are exercises which provide invaluable practice. By the time a student has completed the module, every aspect of the ECDL syllabus will have been covered.

Software used

The instructions and screenshots are based on a PC running Microsoft Windows XP with Internet Explorer 6 and Outlook Express 6. However, it will be relatively easy to adapt the instructions for use with other versions of Windows.

Extra resources

Answers to practice exercises and other useful supporting material can be found on the publisher's web site www.payne-gallway.co.uk/ecdl.

About ECDL

The European Computer Driving Licence (ECDL) is the European-wide qualification enabling people to demonstrate their competence in computer skills. Candidates must study and pass the test for each of the seven modules listed below before they are awarded an ECDL certificate. The ECDL tests must be undertaken at an accredited test centre. For more details of ECDL tests and test centres, visit the ECDL web site www.ecdl.com.

Module 1: Concepts of Information Technology

Module 2: Using the Computer and Managing Files

Module 3: Word Processing

Module 4: Spreadsheets

Module 5: Database

Module 6: Presentation

Module 7: Information and Communication

Module 7

Information and Communication

The module is divided in two sections. The first section, *Information*, will help you to understand some of the concepts and terms associated with using the Internet, and to appreciate the security considerations. You will be able to:

- accomplish common Web search tasks using a Web browser
- use search engine tools
- bookmark web sites
- print web pages
- navigate around and complete web-based forms.

In the second section, *Communication*, you will learn some of the concepts of electronic mail (e-mail), and gain an appreciation of some of the security considerations associated with using e-mail. You will be able to:

- use e-mail software to send and receive messages
- attach files to mail messages
- organise and manage message folders within e-mail software.

Module **7**   Table of Contents

Browsing

The Internet

The Internet consists of a huge number of computers connected together all over the world. While a small group of connected computers constitutes a network, the Internet is an **Inter**national **net**work of networks. Once connected, you can use the Internet to send e-mails or browse the Web.

The World Wide Web is the best-known part of the Internet. It consists of hundreds of millions of web pages stored on computers the world over, which you can access from your computer. Most large companies and organisations have a web site and so do more and more private individuals.

Web Browser software

To view web pages, you need a type of software called a **browser**. One of the most common browsers is **Microsoft Internet Explorer** which we shall use in this book.

The browser will not be able to show pages unless the computer is connected to an **Internet Service Provider** or **ISP**. ISPs include BT, AOL, Demon and thousands of others worldwide. When you connect your computer to the Internet, you connect to an ISP's computer which stores and transmits data to other ISPs and thus to other users. Your connection will either be permanent or dial-up.

To start Internet Explorer:

◉   *Either* double-click the icon for Internet Explorer. This is next to the **Start** button.

◉   *Or* click **Start**, **Programs**, then **Internet Explorer.**

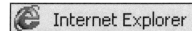
Internet Explorer

◉   A dialogue box may ask if you want to connect: enter your username and password and click **Connect**.

A web page will now appear on the screen. This is probably a page that was set as a **default** by your ISP or computer manufacturer. In Chapter 7.3 you will find out how to change this.

Entering an address

You can go to a different page by entering another address.

▶ Click in the Address bar at the top of the screen. The text will be highlighted.

Click in here then type. This will overwrite existing text

Go

▶ Type in **www.bbc.co.uk** and click on the **Go** button or press **Enter**.

This should bring up the BBC web site at the opening or **home** page. It will look similar to the picture below, but not identical since most people and companies are continually changing their web sites.

Click here to scroll down

Web pages may be longer than the screen – like this one. To see the whole page, either click in the scroll bar or press the **Page Down** key. **Ctrl-End** takes you to the bottom of the page, **Ctrl-Home** back to the top.

Tip:

If you are looking for something on the page, choose **Find** (**on This Page**) from the **Edit** menu and enter the word or phrase.

Navigating the Web

Most web pages have **hot links** – also called **hypertext** links or **hyperlinks** – which enable you to jump to another page, or back to the top of the same page if it's quite long. When you move the mouse pointer around the screen, the shape changes from an arrow to a hand when it is over a hot area. These are usually text underlined in blue but may also be pictures.

When you click on a hot area, the browser jumps to a new page.

▶ Click on the **History** link in the middle of the page.

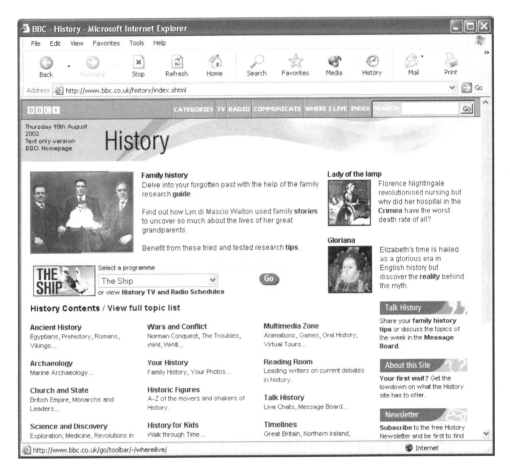

The History page lets you view the past from many different aspects, and there are numerous other links as well.

Tip:

The page may look quite different when you come to look at it but there should still be something of interest.

▶ Click on **Timelines** and see what comes up.

Returning to a previous page

To go back to the previous page:

◑   Click on the **Back** button at the left of the toolbar.

◑   Click **Back** repeatedly until you are back at the home page.

Notice that the links you have already clicked have changed colour to remind you that you've been there.

◑   Now try clicking the **Forward** button.

Notice this takes you forward through the pages you were going back through. It is greyed out unless you were going back.

Both buttons have a down-arrow – you can click on it and choose a page from the list.

Tip:
You can also use the **Alt** key with left or right arrow for **Back** and **Forward**. Clicking the mouse wheel also sends you **Back**.

Bookmarking a web page

To save having to remember how to return to a page you can **bookmark** it by adding it to a list of favourite sites.

◑   Go back to the BBC home page.

◑   From the menu bar choose **Favorites**, **Add to Favorites** and click **OK**.

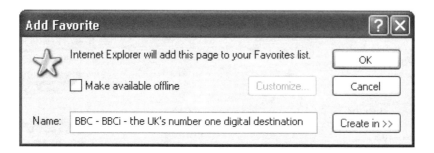

Tip:
You can also create your own folders to put entries in.

The web page address

Every web page has a unique address known as the **URL** – for Uniform Resource Locator. This has distinct parts separated by dots, each part having a special significance. A typical address is:

http://www.bbc.co.uk

http:// (Hypertext Transfer Protocol) is the protocol (set of rules) used by the Internet for sending and receiving data between computers. Some addresses may have **https://** for a secure (protected) page with sensitive information. **ftp://** (File Transfer Protocol) is another protocol which is used for transferring files.

There's no need to type in **http://** as the browser adds it automatically.

www means World Wide Web and is in most but not all web page addresses.

bbc.co.uk is the **domain name** showing the organisation owning the site and has several parts.

co is the type of site, in this case a commercial organisation. International company domain names generally end in **.com**.

Some other codes are **gov** for government, **org** for non-profit organisations, **ac** for educational sites (**edu** in the USA), or **sch** for schools.

If the site is neither **.com** nor US-based there is usually a country code – **uk** for the UK, **fr** for France, **de** for Germany, **es** for Spain, **it** for Italy, **ch** for Switzerland, **ie** for Ireland, and so on.

There may also be the name of a file on the end of the address (after a slash) such as **/index.htm**. Web pages are written in a language called **HTML** (for **Hypertext Markup Language**) and each page is a file usually ending in **.htm**.

Here are some sample web addresses – you can probably guess who they belong to.

www.disney.com	www.cam.ac.uk	www.bmw.de
www.nationalgallery.org.uk	www.harvard.edu	www.louvre.fr
www.worldwildlife.org	www.nasa.gov	www.lastampa.it

Entering an address from the address bar

The address box in the address bar has a down-arrow at the right-hand end. If you click on this, a list opens below with the URLs of recently visited web pages.

○ Click on one and notice the browser jumps to that page.

We'll now go back to the BBC home page. Instead of using the **Back** button, here's another way.

○ Start typing the URL **www.bbc.co.uk/history**

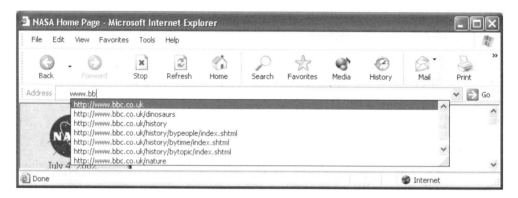

As soon as you get to **www.b** Internet Explorer now lists all the addresses matching what you have typed.

> **Tip:**
> If this doesn't happen, look up AutoComplete in the index.

○ Select the address in the list.

Returning to a bookmarked page

For a quick way to return to the BBC home page, you could either use the **Back** button again or find it in Favorites where you saved it earlier.

○ Click the **Favorites** button on the toolbar.

○ Click the item in the Favorites pane on the left, to bring up that page.

○ Click the **Favorites** button again to hide the pane.

Refreshing a web page

The browser stores the pages you browse in a file known as a **cache** on your hard disk. If you ask for the same page again, it is the stored page that is opened: if you are not sure whether you are looking at the latest version of the page, or you get a message that a web page cannot be displayed, click the **Refresh** button. This then reloads the page from the Internet, not from the cache.

Using Help functions

If you want more information on, say, how to delete pages held in cache, or assign more disk space to cache, you could do worse than look at the Help system in Internet Explorer.

◉   Click on the **Help** menu, **Contents and Index**.

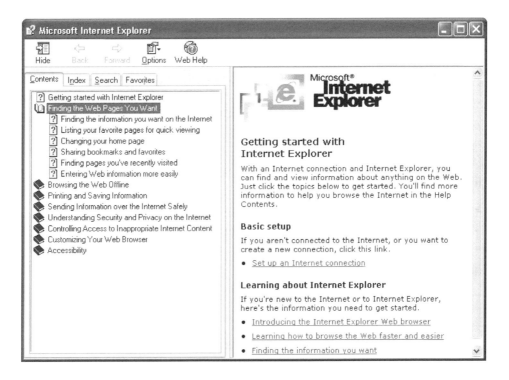

Tip:
You could press the **F1** key to access Help instead.

The topics are marked by Book icons: clicking on a topic lists the items below.

◉   Click on an item to see the associated help information on the right.

You can also search the help index by entering a keyword.

◉   Click the **Index** tab and type **cache**.

Back returns
you to the
previous topic

To change
or print the
display

Hides or
shows the
left-hand
pane

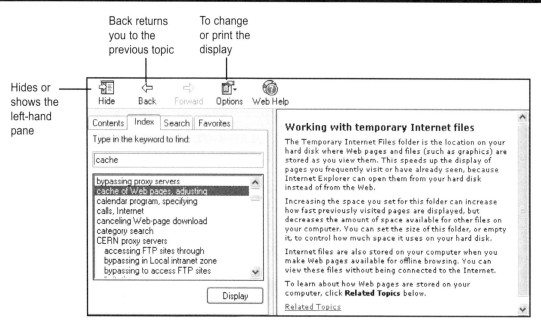

This lists the related topics; you click on one to show the help on the right. Alternatively you can enter your keyword on the **Search** tab. If all else fails there is also Microsoft online help from the **Web Help** button.

◉   Close the Help window when you have seen enough.

Stopping a page downloading

If a page is taking too long to open (the mouse pointer keeps showing an hour-glass), click the **Stop** button. This often happens if a page has a lot of pictures.

Missing page

You may find that your browser cannot find a page although you clicked on a link to it, and it displays something like this.

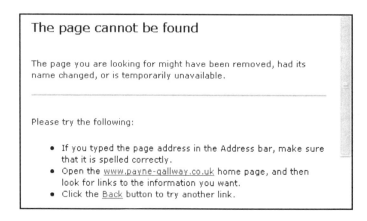

Don't worry, this often happens! The Internet is growing so fast that many web pages have mistakes in their link addresses. This may be because the page that a link points to has been removed or had its address changed. It could also be due to a problem with the site server or because of heavy demand for that site.

Tip:
You'll see a similar message if you type an address in wrongly and the browser can't find it.

Ending an Internet session

◉   Close Internet Explorer by clicking the Close icon (**X**) at the top right of your screen, or by selecting **File, Close** from the menu bar.

If you have a dial-up connection you should disconnect as soon as you have finished since being on the Internet uses your phone line. Note that closing Internet Explorer does not automatically disconnect you – you have to instruct the computer to disconnect.

While you are connected, the **Dial-up** icon appears in the Status bar at bottom right of the screen.

   ◉   Right-click the Dial-up icon and select **Disconnect**.

Exercises

1.   Open Internet Explorer and make sure you are connected to the Internet.

2.   Enter the URL **www.bbc.co.uk/music**

3.   Find on this page all instances of the word **jazz**.

4.   Bookmark this page.

5.   Go to the site **www.multimap.com** and bookmark it.

6.   Enter your postcode to display a small-scale map of your home area.

7.   Click the **Print** button to print out the map.

8.   Disconnect from the Internet if you have a dial-up connection.

9.   Close Internet Explorer.

Search Engines

Using a search engine

As you can see, it's easy to spend hours browsing the Web, jumping aimlessly from page to page. Some web sites – like the BBC – have a search box to find things on that site, but to look up a particular topic anywhere on the Web you can use a **search engine**. There are several well-known search engines such as Google, Yahoo, AltaVista and Ask Jeeves. A search engine is software which enables you to find information on almost any conceivable topic, from holidays to university courses, best deals on electronic goods to groceries, long-lost friends to dating agencies.

> Load Internet Explorer by double-clicking the icon.

> Click in the Address box and enter the address **www.google.com**

> Add it to Favorites.

Search engines usually have directories, news, local events and information but you can also search by entering a **keyword**.

Searching by keyword

Google allows you to type a word or phrase, and then comes back with a list of related web pages. Suppose you wanted to find the Prime Minister's official web site.

○ Type **10 Downing Street** into the search box and click the **Google Search** button.

Google comes back with a list of links to **www.number-10.gov.uk** of which the home page is at the top.

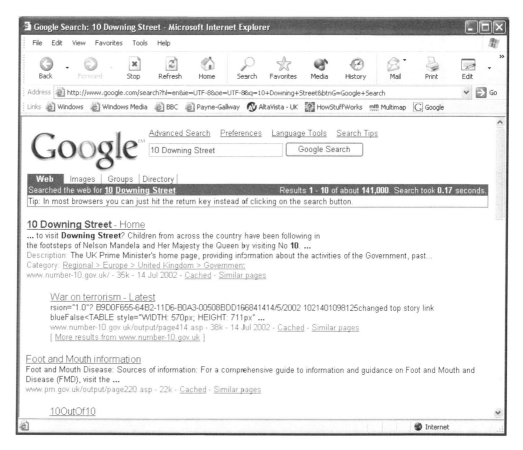

○ Click the first link to admire the Number 10 site.

The Google results are consistently so relevant that they provide an alternative button **I'm Feeling Lucky** which takes you straight to the first result without seeing the list. In this case, this would have been all you needed!

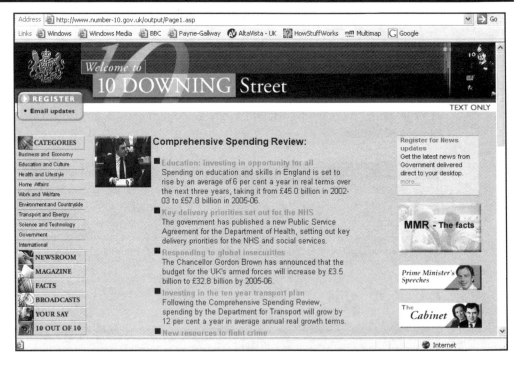

▶   Go back to the Google home page.

Time for another search. Suppose we wanted a cooking recipe for salsa.

▶   In the search box, enter **salsa** and click **Google Search**.

This finds a huge number of references but mostly for dance, music or cycles! Some are not in English.

We need to refine the search by including sauces and recipes and excluding music, dance and cycles.

Including and excluding pages

We can tell Google to exclude topics we don't want by adding a keyword with a minus in front. Similarly, if we are particularly interested in a topic – such as sauces and recipes – we can add keywords with a plus in front.

▶   Try adding **–music –dance –cycle +recipe** and click **Google Search**.

This is better, but you might be interested only in tomato, chilli or bean.

◉ Add **+tomato OR chili OR bean** to the search string.

Here the OR must be in capitals. This will narrow the results further.

Tip:
Similarly if you wanted to specify a chili bean recipe, you would put chili AND bean. You can also specify a phrase in quotes, such as "salsa recipe". For UK sites only, specify **site:.uk**

It is often convenient to open a web page in a new window so that you can compare pages. To do this, Shift-click on the link, or right-click and choose **Open in New Window**. If you want to open several web pages at a time, each in a new window, use **File**, **New**, **Window**.

Searching by directories

Many search engines and some other sites have information arranged by topic in categories. To see this:

◉ Go to the **Google** home page and click the **Directory** button.　**Directory**

Arts	**Home**	**Regional**
Movies, Music, Television,...	Consumers, Homeowners, Family,...	Asia, Europe, North America,...
Business	**Kids and Teens**	**Science**
Industries, Finance, Jobs,...	Computers, Entertainment, School,...	Biology, Psychology, Physics,...
Computers	**News**	**Shopping**
Hardware, Internet, Software,...	Media, Newspapers, Current Events,...	Autos, Clothing, Gifts,...
Games	**Recreation**	**Society**
Board, Roleplaying, Video,...	Food, Outdoors, Travel,...	Issues, People, Religion,...
Health	**Reference**	**Sports**
Alternative, Fitness, Medicine,...	Education, Libraries, Maps,...	Basketball, Football, Soccer,...

This shows lists of categories which in turn have subcategories so that you can gradually home in on what you are looking for. If you were interested for example in scuba diving you would click on **Recreation, Outdoors, Scuba Diving** and then choose **Underwater Photography** or some other aspect.

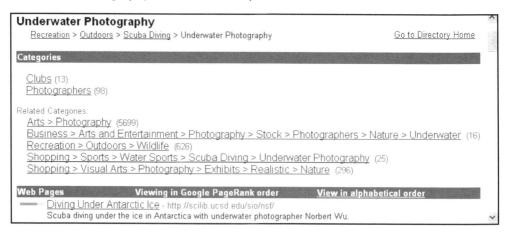

Directories, of which the best example is Open Directory Project **(www.dmoz.org)**, are compiled by hand so the information is always relevant. Search engines on the other hand keep an index of keywords which is added to by special programs – known as **spiders** or **crawlers** – which continually search the web collecting references but these may not always be relevant.

Other search engines

There are numerous other search engines, with more appearing constantly.

For simple straightforward queries, **Ask Jeeves (www.ask.co.uk)** invites you to use **natural language** – that is, plain English.

Rather than reply instantly, Jeeves presents you with related questions (hand-compiled) using dropdown menus which will hopefully lead you to the answer, and you'll probably find other interesting things along the way.

Whatever the query, whether used cars or train times, Jeeves is immediately on the case with a list of helpful suggestions.

Tip:

A few search engines – known as **meta search engines** – submit your keywords to several search engines at once, and pass you the results. Look at **www.metor.com**

Some search engines (AltaVista but not Google) allow 'wildcards' to cater for variations in words. Thus **compan*** will find **company**, **companies**, **companion**, etc.

◉ Look at AltaVista **www.altavista.co.uk**

◉ Use AltaVista to find your dream home somewhere in the UK.

This is Powis Castle on the National Trust web site.

Duplicating text

Suppose you want to copy some of the text and graphics from this web site into a **Word** document.

○   Make sure you have **Word** running and if you don't have a blank document open choose **File, New**.

○   Go back to **Internet Explorer** (press **Alt-Tab**) or select it from the Task bar at the bottom of the screen.

○   Drag to select a few lines of text (or the URL in the address bar).

○   From the **Edit** menu, choose **Copy**.

○   Go back to Word and from the **Edit** menu, choose **Paste**.

Note:
You may only copy for your own personal use. Copyright material may not be reproduced without permission.

Duplicating graphics

It is better to copy the graphics separately from the text.

○   In **Internet Explorer**, right-click on the picture you want to copy and select **Copy**.

○   Return to Word, right-click on the document and select **Paste**.

Tip:
The image in your document may only be a link to the web page it came from, and will disappear when the computer is no longer online. To avoid this, select the image and press **Ctrl-Shift-F9**.

In Word, you'll need to right-click the picture and choose **Format Picture**, **Layout** to get the picture alongside the text.

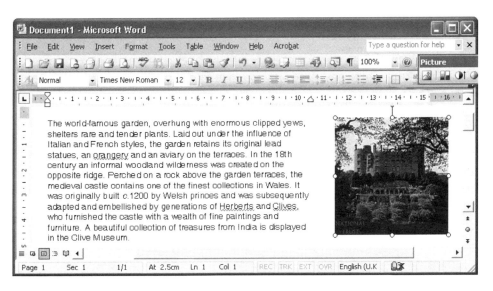

In this case, the picture was held on the clipboard. To save a web site picture as a file, right-click it, choose **Save Picture As** and browse to the folder you want to put it in.

 In Internet Explorer 6 when you hover the mouse over an image, the Image toolbar should appear which allows you to save, print or e-mail the image.

Saving a web page

You can save a web page to look at later.

> ○ In the browser, choose **File**, **Save As**, select a folder and type **Castle** as the file name. Set **Web Page**, **htm** as the file type and click **OK**.

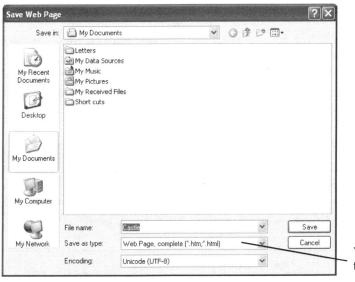

You can save it as text or html

This saves the page on your hard disk as a .htm file which can be opened later with the browser. You can also save it as text only if you don't want any graphics.

Printing a web page

You can print an entire web page simply by clicking the **Print** button, or by selecting **File**, **Print**. There are some print options to change the page margins and orientation.

◉ Choose **File**, **Page Setup**.

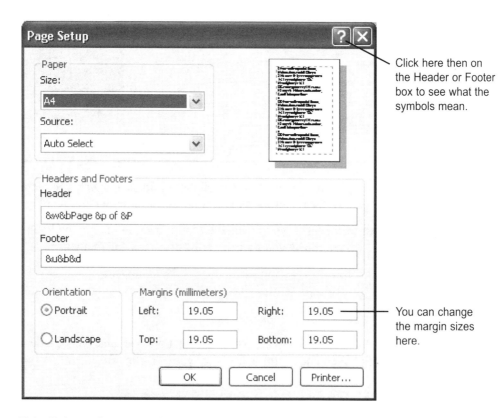

Click here then on the Header or Footer box to see what the symbols mean.

You can change the margin sizes here.

This dialogue lets you select the paper size and whether you want the page printed vertically (**portrait**) or horizontally (**landscape**), as well as the top, bottom, left and right margin sizes. The printed page will have details such as the page title, date and time at the top and bottom but you can change these and add text of your own using the symbols in the Header and Footer boxes.

Tip:

Try using **context help** to see what these symbols mean: click the **?** button at the top right of the window, then in the Header box.

◉ Select **File**, **Print Preview** and preview the printed page(s). From the toolbar at the top you can zoom in or out, browse the pages or print.

○ Select **Print** on the preview window or close it and choose **File, Print**.

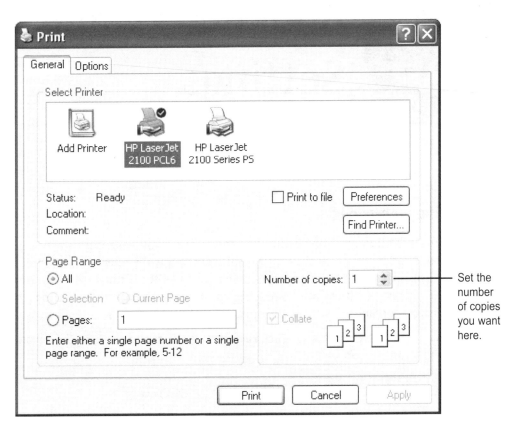

Here you can print the whole web page – which may extend to several printed pages – or particular pages, or just a part that you have selected which avoids wasting ink and paper on almost empty pages. Similarly for web pages built with frames you can print individual frames from the **Options** tab.

Exercises

1. Open Internet Explorer and make sure you are connected to the Internet.

2. Go to **www.google.com**

3. Use search keywords to list web sites about Leonardo (da Vinci).

4. Open a site in a new browser page.

5. Print out a selected area of a page containing relevant information.

6. Save the page as a **.htm** file.

7. Copy some text and a picture into a new Word document and save the document.

8. Close Internet Explorer.

Bookmarks and Settings

Bookmarking web pages

You will often find you need to go back to pages you have visited previously and bookmarking is a way of keeping your most frequently-used sites in a list, for easy recall. In Internet Explorer this is called the **Favorites** list and it is very useful when you are working on a project. Sometimes you will want to delete items from the **Favorites** list or reorganise it so that the most used sites are near the top of the list.

○　In **Internet Explorer**, click **Favorites** on the toolbar. Notice the **Favorites** list opens on the left.

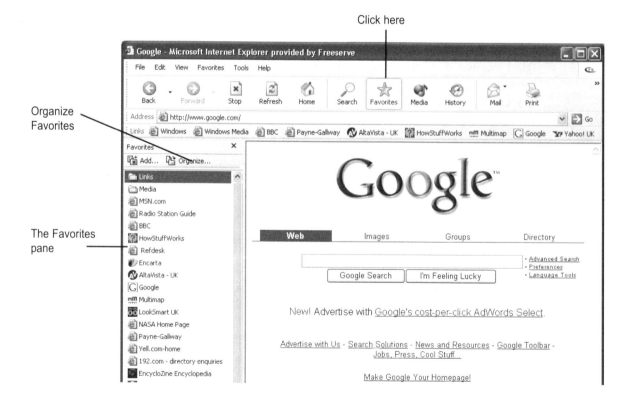

You can ignore some of the ones at the top which may be to do with your Internet provider (in this case Freeserve), and you may also have **My Documents** which is where Windows puts your **Word** files. You can now choose a web page from the list and display it.

The entries in the **Favorites** list appear in the order that they were added. You may want to change the order, perhaps moving the most useful ones up to the top.

○ Click on **Organize Favorites** at the top of the Favorites pane or select **Favorites, Organize Favorites**.

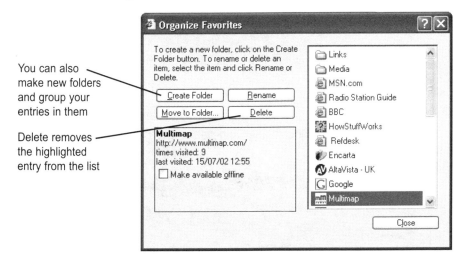

You can also make new folders and group your entries in them

Delete removes the highlighted entry from the list

Tip:
To change the order of items in the list, just drag them up or down. To remove an unwanted entry, select it and click the **Delete** button.

Creating a bookmark folder

As the list builds up, it is advisable to group the entries in specific folders.

○ Click the **Create Folder** button and type the name for your folder, for example, **Reference**.

○ Click **Close** to close the window and you should now see the new folder.

Adding web pages to a bookmark folder

You can now move entries to the folder or add them to it directly.

○ Select an entry in the **Favorites** list and click **Move to Folder**.

○ Select the new folder and click **OK**.

○ Close the **Organize Favorites** window.

To add a new web site directly to the Reference folder:

○ Enter the URL for Encarta encyclopedia (**http://encarta.msn.co.uk**).

Tip:
Notice not all addresses have **www**.

○ Choose **Favorites**, **Add to Favorites** then **Create In**, select the **Reference** folder and click **OK**.

○ Hide the **Favorites** window by clicking the **Favorites** button on the toolbar to deselect it.

The History list

Internet Explorer keeps track of all the pages you have visited and when. This is kept in the **History** list.

○ Click on the **History** icon in the toolbar and notice the History list pane opens on the left.

Click here

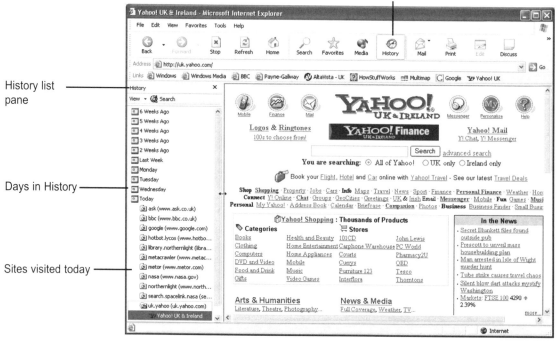

History list pane

Days in History

Sites visited today

The **History** list lets you view the sites that you (or someone else) have visited recently. In the list, the pages visited are grouped by day. Clicking on an icon expands or contracts it, and selecting a link displays the page.

○ Click on the icon for **Today** to expand it (if not already) and see the sites you have visited today.

As well as viewing the **History** list by date, you can also order it by **Site** or by **Most Visited**.

Deleting the browse history

How far back your History goes depends on how your browser is set up – this one is 6 weeks. To delete the History list:

◉ From the **Tools** menu select **Internet Options**.

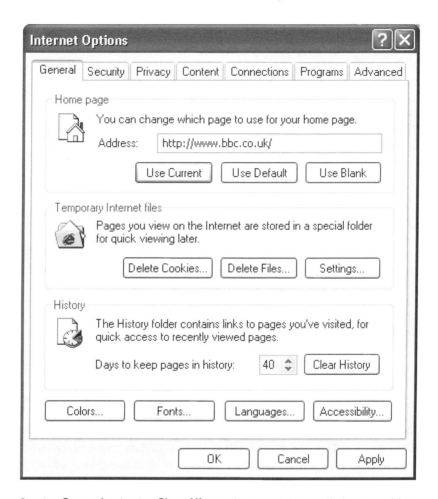

On the **General** tab, the **Clear History** button deletes all the stored history links.

Changing your start page

It is inconvenient to have Internet Explorer open with a site that is of little interest, particularly if it takes a long time to load. This can be easily changed from the **General** tab shown above.

◉ Go to the page you would like to come up, say the BBC home page.

◉ From the **Tools** menu select **Internet Options**.

◉ Click **Use Current**.

Loading pages without images

If you have a slow connection you can speed things up by downloading the text without the pictures on a web site. On the Internet Options **Advanced** tab, scroll down to **Multimedia** and uncheck **Show Pictures**.

> ⚙ Multimedia
>   ☐ Don't display online media content in the media bar
>   ☑ Enable Automatic Image Resizing
>   ☑ Enable Image Toolbar (requires restart)
>   ☑ Play animations in web pages
>   ☑ Play sounds in web pages
>   ☑ Play videos in web pages
>   ☐ Show image download placeholders
>   ☑ Show pictures

 —— Each image position on the page is now marked by an icon.

Address box autocomplete

If, as you enter an address, the browser tries to complete the address for you instead of showing a list of matching addresses beneath, uncheck **Use Inline AutoComplete** in the Browsing section on the Internet Options **Advanced** tab.

☐ Use inline AutoComplete

Displaying and hiding built-in toolbars

Internet Explorer has certain settings made by **default** – as set by Microsoft or the supplier – but these can be changed. The **Standard Buttons** toolbar, **Address Bar** and **Links Bar** can be shown and hidden either from the **View** menu or by right-clicking a toolbar. The **Links Bar** appears either at the end of the Address bar or below it (if on the right, you can drag it down).

The Links bar is very versatile – you can drag an address onto it from the Address bar and drag the addresses along to rearrange them. Try it! You can delete or rename them by right-clicking and choosing from the menu.

Items on the Links Bar come from the Links folder which appears in **Favorites** and you can add a new site directly to it. The Status Bar at the bottom of the screen is also selected from the **View** menu.

You can make a web page as large as possible using **View**, **Full Screen** or pressing **F11**. This takes up the entire screen except for the toolbar icons. F11 returns you to normal mode.

Exercises

1. Open Internet Explorer and show the Favorites pane.

2. Click **Organize Favorites**.

3. Create a new bookmark folder called **Shopping**.

4. Go to **www.amazon.co.uk** and add it to the new folder.

5. Go to **www.192.com**, **www.royalmail.com** and **www.yell.com** and add them to the Links bar.

6. Close Internet Explorer.

Downloading Files

You can download pictures, video clips, sounds and software from the Internet. In this chapter you will learn how to find and save pictures and software.

You'll need to keep them in separate folders where they can easily be found again when you need them. If you don't know how to make a new folder, refer to Module 2.

Looking for pictures

The Internet has lots of pictures you can download. Some are copyright but many are free. Let's find something brightly coloured, say a kingfisher.

○ Open **Internet Explorer** and connect to the Internet.

○ Open the **Favorites list** and choose **AltaVista**.

○ Click on **Images**.

You can choose several types of image from UK or worldwide. Suppose we wanted to see colour photos of birds.

Click
here

○ Fill in the details as shown above and click **Search**.

AltaVista returns a few hundred images. Many of them are are not free to copy – a popup message may warn you of this when you run the mouse pointer over them, otherwise clicking on an image will give further details.

○ Find a suitable image.

11398091.jpg ──────── Images are .jpg or .gif.

This is the number of ───────**256x170 8 KB**──────── This is the file size
'picture elements' or   of this 'thumbnail'
pixels   image

> **Tip:**
> Images from **Corbis** (**www.corbis.com**) are free to copy if they are watermarked and some are also royalty-free: check on the site. Also try **www.freeimages.co.uk**

◉ To copy the picture, right-click it and choose **Save Picture As**.

◉ Give the picture a name and save the file in the folder you created, or another suitable one.

◉ You can try clicking the picture to see it at a larger size.

If you don't like these, check the next **Results** pages. You can also enter **royalty-free** as a search keyword! There are also images on **Google**.

> **Tip:**
> Once you've saved a lot of image files, a graphic viewer program is useful to browse them. We shall see one later in this chapter.

Using a downloaded graphic

You can now open the file in a graphics package, or put it in a **Word** document (using **Insert, Picture, From File**).

Picture files on web pages are usually stored in either **.jpg** (pronounced jay-peg) or **.gif** (pronounced as in gift) format since these are compressed, giving small files which are quick to load. These files lose some quality in the compression process so are not very high **resolution** – a bit 'dotty' like a newspaper photograph.

Downloading sounds

AltaVista offers sounds and music in different formats. For some files, Windows may prompt you to download special software.

Warning:
Some sounds may be copyright

○ Still in AltaVista, select **MP3/Audio**, enter a keyword and click **Search**.

The downloadable sounds are shown – something like this.

<u>Humpback Whale Song</u>

| **Filename:** | humpsong.wav | **Upload Date:** | 10-MAR-96 |
| **File size:** | 460222 bytes | **File Owner:** | Jim Cara |

Description: WAV File: "Sounds of a Humpback Whale Singing: To hear this WAV file you will need a Sound Card or PC Speaker Driver Program. You must have software capable of playing WAV files

---

Sounds can be played using **Windows Media Player**. In Internet Explorer 6 you can click the **Media** button to open it as a pane in the Internet Explorer screen.

Tip:
You can open Media Player on its own from **Start**, **Programs**, **Accessories**.

○ Click the **Media** button if you have it, then click on the sound file.

Click to play a sound again

You can copy the file by right-clicking on the icon and choosing **Save Target As**, which will prompt you for which folder to put it in.

Windows Media Player will play all types of sound files, including music compressed as MP3. Some links simply play a sound file without downloading it – a process known as **streaming**. Many sites offer this.

Downloading video clips

These are available in several formats on the **Video Clips** tab. You may be prompted to download special software such as **RealPlayer** or **Quicktime**. Files tend to be large and the effect can be jerky without a fast machine. Video can also be streamed.

Downloading text files

Some search engines allow you to search for specific types of file. Click the **Advanced Search** link in Google and try entering **tiger** as the keyword and **.doc** as the file type. This lists doc files only; click a link and specify the folder to put it in. Alternatively, go to **www.payne-gallway.co.uk/ecdl** and download a .doc file.

Downloading software

There's a lot of software available on the Internet and a good site is **Tucows**.

In the **Address** box enter **http://tucows.blueyonder.co.uk** and click **Go**.

Tip:
This is a **mirror site** (local provider) for **www.tucows.com**.

Programs are either for sale, **shareware** (you try before you buy), **freeware** or demonstrations (both free). Software for Windows is arranged by category. We are going to download some freeware – an image viewer to look at your pictures!

○ First make a new folder called **Download** as described in Module 2.

○ Click the **Multimedia** tab, look for **Image Viewers** and scroll down the list to IrfanView.

Tip:
There may be a link direct to it as shown above. If you can't find it, enter the name in the **Search** box.

You will see something like this. Programs have a 'cow rating'- from 1 to 5!

Irfan View 3.75	**July 14th,**	**Freeware**	🐄🐄🐄🐄🐄	808.0K	**Windows 95/98**
This feature-rich image viewer and converter supports many formats.	2002				Windows Me
					Windows NT
					Windows 2000
					Windows XP

○ Click the appropriate link on the right for your version of Windows.

A dialogue asks whether you want to open it or save it.

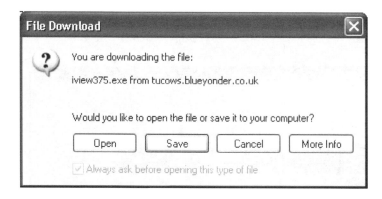

○ Choose **Save**. In the Save As dialogue, go to your **Download** folder then click **Save**.

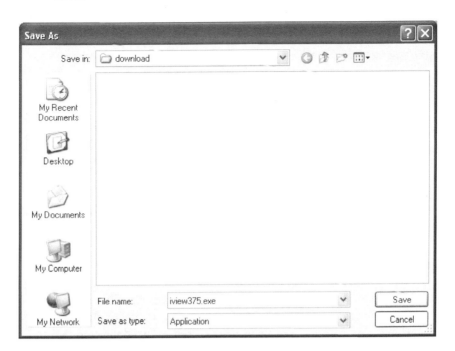

The file downloads, taking about 3 minutes with a dial-up connection.

Tip:
To see how the download is going using a modem, hold the mouse pointer over the **Dial-Up** icon. A status message pops up.

○ Once complete, click **Open Folder** to show the downloaded file in your folder.

Warning:
Check the size of the file is about 800Kb; if not the download may have broken off. If nothing happens when you double-click the file, try downloading again.

The program can now be installed.

○ Double-click the file in the folder and the install screen should appear.

○ Without changing any settings, click **Next** on each screen, then **Done**.

The program is now installed and you can run it from the **Start**, **Programs** menu or by double-clicking the icon on the desktop.

Tip:
When downloading a large file, if the connection breaks you then have to start again. Using a **download manager** such as **GetRight** (www.getright.com) not only lets you interrupt the download but automatically resumes if the connection breaks.

Executable files

When you download a program file, it will have a name ending in **.exe** meaning it is an **executable** file. The program may install itself and start running automatically. Some **.exe** files are not the program file itself but a compressed or **zipped** version shrunk for faster downloading. The file is self-extracting. To expand or **unzip** it:

○ Make a new folder.

○ Find the file and copy it into the folder.

Tip:
Hold down the **Ctrl** key and drag the file to copy it.

○ Double-click on the file, **Browse** to the target folder then **Unzip**.

The original and much larger file will now be in the folder. If it too is a **.exe** file, double-click on it to install or run the program.

Reading .pdf files

Sometimes documents you download have names ending in .pdf – for **Portable Document Format**. To read them, you need a program called **Acrobat Reader**. If it's not on your machine you can download it free from **www.adobe.com**

Tip:
Once Acrobat Reader is installed on your computer, you just double-click a .pdf file in Windows Explorer to open it.

Viruses

There is a risk that a file you download (or copy from a floppy disk) could be infected with a virus – a piece of computer code that can have various effects ranging from mischief to damaging your computer. Make sure you have Virus Checker software installed to catch the viruses as they arrive.

If you are on a network, it should already be protected.

Exercises

1.   Open Internet Explorer.

2.   Use AltaVista to download a royalty-free sound file.

3.   Use Google to download a few royalty-free image files.

4.   Open the IrfanView application downloaded previously and use it to display the image files.

Shopping and Security

You can use the Internet for buying numerous things and it's also an invaluable consumer guide. You pay by credit card but provided that you enter the payment details on a secure site – with an address beginning **https://** – it's as safe as the high street. Let's take a look.

Completing a web-based form

One of the most developed online sites is Tesco's. There's the impressive range of foodstuffs and you can order videos, books, electrical goods, home furnishings and babyware. You can arrange your personal finances (mortgage, insurance, ISAs, credit cards, loans), order currencies if you're travelling and have flowers delivered.

▶ Go to the site **www.tesco.com**

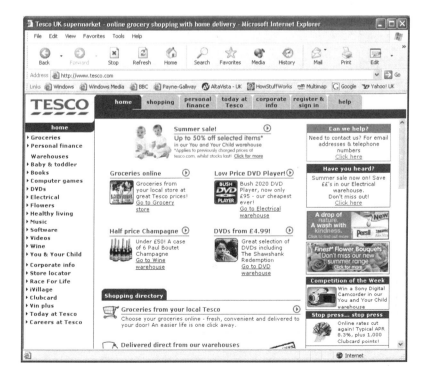

This is a **protected site** requiring you to register on your first visit and thereafter sign in with your username and password.

◉   Click on the **Register & sign-in** tab.

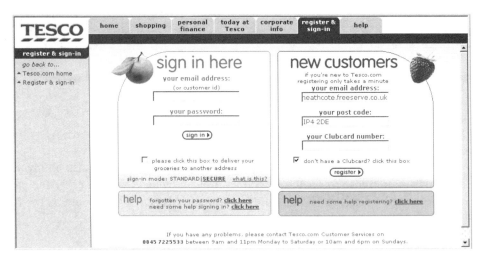

◉   Enter your e-mail address and post code, click **register** and give yourself a password.

You are immediately given a clubcard number – keep this handy with your password and proceed to the online grocery. Here you just browse the list, enter the quantities and click **Add to Basket**.

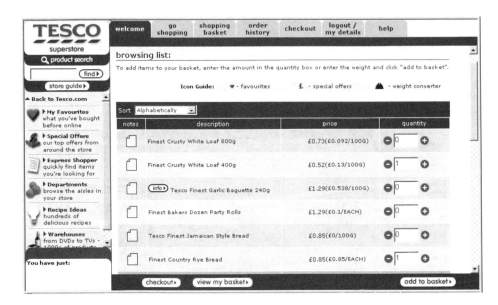

You can look at other sections from the Store Guide on the left, view your basket so far and change any quantities. This is called an **interactive form**, which constantly updates itself as you enter or change values.

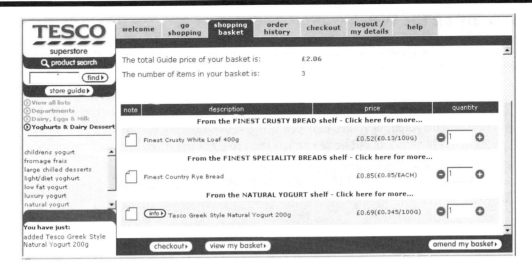

Having chosen what you need from all sections, you now click on **Checkout**, and book a delivery slot.

You are now required to give away sensitive information – your credit card details – and this is done on a secure page with an address beginning **https://**.

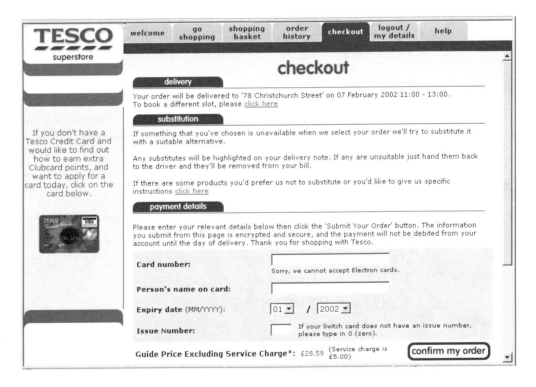

And that's all there is to it!

Security on the Web

When using a web site you are sometimes open to fraud: a site may not be who it says it is in order to obtain credit card information.

A secure page with an **https://** address has a **Digital Certificate** (granted by a **Certificate Authority**) confirming that the site is secure and genuine. Information is exchanged via **encrypted** messages encoded using keys so that only authorised people can read it. The site sends its **public key** which the recipient uses together with its **private key** to encode the message.

Cookies

These are small files that web sites put on your computer to save your previous settings and preferences for their site and the pages you visited on it. This helps the site customise the view for your next visit, perhaps steering you to other products you might like. Cookies are usually innocent and can only send back information that you provide. Allowing a web site to create a cookie does not give that or any other site access to the rest of your computer, and only the site that created the cookie can read it. This is fine provided that sites do not share the cookie information with others who might, for example, direct specific advertisements at children. Internet Explorer accepts cookies by default but you have some control over them via the **Tools**, **Options**, **Privacy** pane which offers six settings ranging from 'block all' to 'accept all'. On the **General** pane, **Delete Cookies** removes all cookies from your machine.

Firewall

When you are online continuously, it is advisable to install **firewall** software to stop anyone **hacking** into your computer from the outside and copying information or making changes.

Exercises

1. Use Ask Jeeves to find a railway timetable such as **www.nationalrail.co.uk**

2. Use an interactive form to find some sample fares for one adult and one child travelling from Ipswich to Birmingham one way. Note the effect on the cost and journey time of:

> different train companies
>
> time of day
>
> fastest / cheapest
>
> number of changes
>
> railcard

3. Copy the times of a fastest and a cheapest journey into a Word document and save it.

4. Print out selected details.

Sending E-mail

E-mail or electronic mail can be sent over the Internet to anybody who has an **e-mail address**. It arrives almost instantaneously anywhere in the world for the cost of a local call. The recipient picks it up when they are ready.

To use e-mail, you need both an e-mail address and a program to handle it. Both are available free.

Note:
There are two types of e-mail connection – permanent, where you are always online, or dial-up.

E-mail addresses

E-mail addresses are quite like web site addresses and made up in much the same way. The format is always:

username@domain_name

Here, **username** is you and domain_name is either the **Internet Service Provider (ISP)** who gives access to the Internet, or a web site address.

Tip:
Some ISPs you may have heard of are AOL, Demon, Virgin, CompuServe, Hotmail, FreeServe, BTInternet, LineOne, … and more are popping up all the time.

Sam Brown's personal address might look like any of these:

sam.brown@virgin.net

sam-brown@aol.com

sam@brownfamily.demon.co.uk

Alternatively, if you have your own registered web site name, your e-mail address can be a part of the site name – **oliver@payne-gallway.co.uk** for example. This has the advantage that if you switch ISPs your e-mail address remains the same.

An e-mail address has no spaces and is usually all in small letters. It MUST be entered correctly or the message will **bounce** – that is, come back undelivered. Every e-mail address is unique.

Using Outlook Express

The program most often used to handle e-mail is **Microsoft Outlook Express** which comes with **Internet Explorer** and that is what is used in this book.

Note:

Another type of e-mail – **Web-based e-mail** – does not require a special program because you access your e-mail from a web site using the browser. This means you have to be online for longer while you deal with mail but the advantage is you can check your mail from any computer anywhere that's on the Internet – particularly useful when travelling. The most popular web-based e-mail is Microsoft's Hotmail: you open an account – free – on **www.hotmail.com**

Click the **Outlook Express** icon which is usually near the **Start** button, otherwise select **Start**, **Programs**, **Outlook Express**.

If there are other people using your computer, you may need to identify yourself by selecting **File**, **Switch Identity** and choosing your name from a list of users.

The **Outlook Express** window allows you to:

compose messages

send and receive messages

reply to messages

forward messages

print messages

keep contact names in an **Address** book

file old messages in folders.

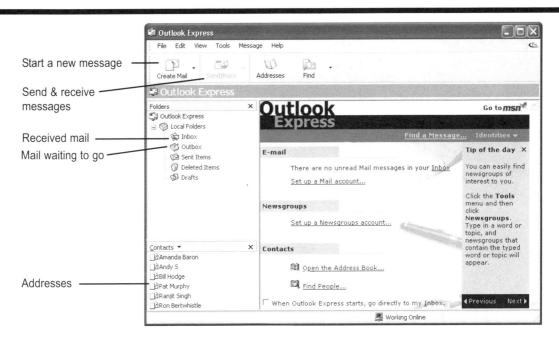

Start a new message

Send & receive messages

Received mail

Mail waiting to go

Addresses

The general window layout can be altered in **View**, **Layout** allowing you to display or hide the built-in toolbars.

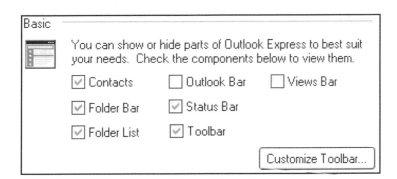

Composing an e-mail

To start a new message to someone you obviously need to know their e-mail address.

O   Click on the **Create Mail** button on the toolbar.

The **New Message** window opens.

O   Type the address in the **To:** box.

O   Leave the **Cc:** box blank. This is used if you want to send a copy of the message to someone else.

O   Type something in the **Subject:** box to say what the message is about.

O   Type the letter in the main window (the message box).

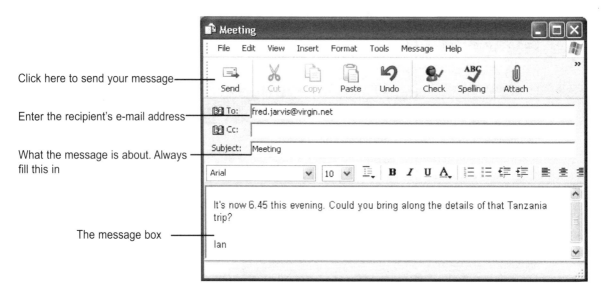

Click here to send your message

Enter the recipient's e-mail address

What the message is about. Always fill this in

The message box

Note:

There are two sending options – sending a message immediately or putting it in the Outbox to send later. For dial-up, the Outbox is better.

○   Select **Tools**, **Options** and on the **Send** tab uncheck **Send messages immediately**.

○   Click the **Send** button on the toolbar.

○   If prompted to **Connect**, click **Cancel**.

The Outbox

The New Message window closes and your message is now in the Outbox. It has not actually been sent yet. You can write messages to several people and store them in the Outbox. When you are ready, you can send them all at once – this uses only a few seconds of online time and saves on the phone bill!

You can look at the contents of the Outbox and edit a message before you send it. You can also delete a message if you change your mind about sending it.

To edit a message in the **Outbox**:

○   Click **Outbox** in the **Folders** pane to select it.

○   Double-click the message header in the **Message List** pane.

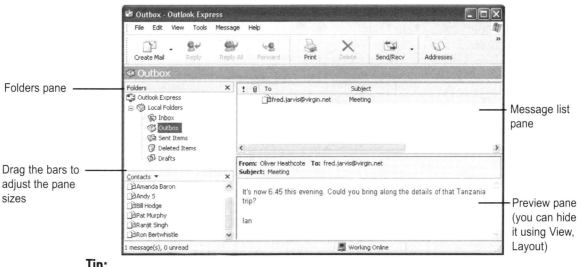

Folders pane

Drag the bars to adjust the pane sizes

Message list pane

Preview pane (you can hide it using View, Layout)

Tip:
Having an **Outbox** means you can write any other messages and send them all at once.

○ An **Edit** window appears and you can edit the message.

○ Click **Send** to put it back in the **Outbox**.

○ If prompted to **Connect**, click **Cancel**.

Help

If you get stuck, try the Help system – choose **Help**, **Contents & Index** or just press the **F1** key.

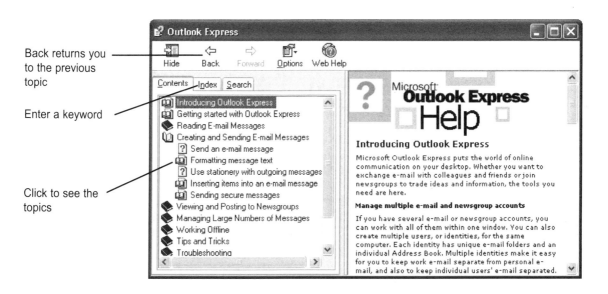

Back returns you to the previous topic

Enter a keyword

Click to see the topics

On the **Contents** tab, you double-click a book symbol to show the topics under the heading. To look up something specific, click the **Index** tab and type in the word or phrase. Outlook Express will list the matching topics.

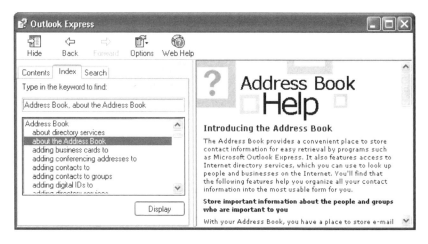

The **Search** tab lists the topics associated with the word you type in.

Some dialogue boxes have the **?** context help button at upper right; click on it then on a part of the dialogue to display extra help. There is also Microsoft online help on the Help menu.

The Address Book

The **Address Book** is used to save the addresses of people you regularly send messages to, so that you don't have to type in their address each time.

Addresses

● Click on the **Addresses** button in the main window.

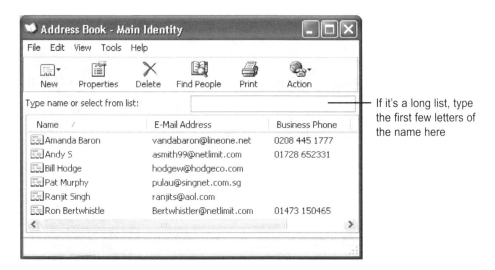

If it's a long list, type the first few letters of the name here

Entering a new address

The **Address Book** window lists any contacts who are already entered. To enter a new contact:

○ Click on the **New** button on the toolbar and choose **New Contact** from the dropdown menu.

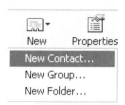

The **Properties** window stores the e-mail, home, and other details of each contact.

○ On the **Name** tab, enter the **First:** and **Last:** names and **Title:**, with **Middle:** and **Nickname:** as well if you like.

○ Click the arrow on the **Display:** box and choose how you want the name displayed.

○ Enter an e-mail address.

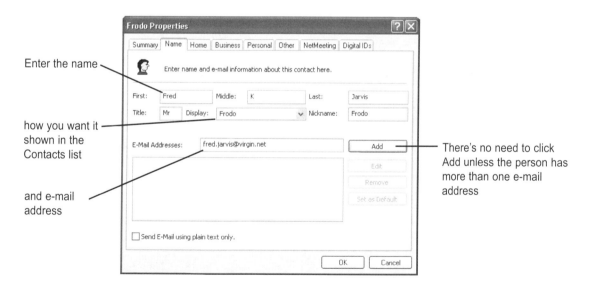

Enter the name —

how you want it
shown in the
Contacts list

and e-mail
address

There's no need to click
Add unless the person has
more than one e-mail
address

○ Click **OK** to enter the address.

The name is now listed in the **Address Book** window.

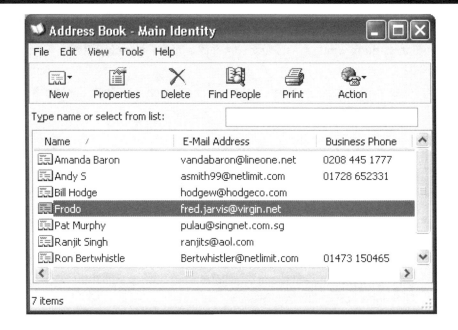

Tip:
You can remove an entry with the **Delete** button.

If you need to change it, say to add the home address:

○   Select the name in the list and click the **Properties** button.

○   On the **Home** tab, enter the details and click **OK**.

The Properties window lets you keep all sorts of details and is very useful

○   Now enter two more addresses and close the address book.

Tip:
You can also set up a **group** of recipients (**New** button, **New Group**) and select the contacts to go into it for a group mailing. With **New Folder** you can start a new list.

Using the Address Book

You can now enter addresses straight from the address book when you send a message.

○   In the **Outlook Express** main window, click **Create Mail**.

○   In the New Message window, click on the icon to the left of **To:** (instead of in the box).

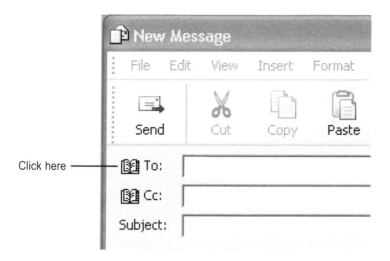

Click here

The **Select Recipients** window opens.

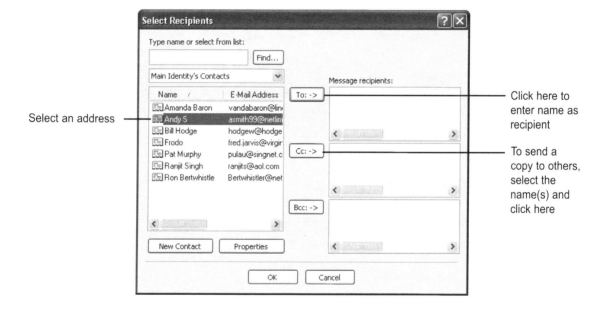

Select an address

Click here to enter name as recipient

To send a copy to others, select the name(s) and click here

Selecting recipients

In the **Select Recipients** window:

○ Select an entry in the **Name** list and click on **To: ->** to transfer it to the **Message Recipients** list.

In the same way you can send a copy of your message to someone else just to keep them posted.

◉   Select another entry in the **Name** list and click on **Cc: ->** to copy it over.

Note:
Cc stands for **Carbon copy**. When the recipients read a message, they can all see who else got it too. To send someone a copy without the other recipients knowing, enter their name in the **Bcc: ->** box. (This stands for **Blind carbon copy**). The Bcc recipients also do not know about each other.

◉   Click on **OK** to return to the **New Message** window.

The recipients are all selected now.

Tip:
Bcc is not usually shown unless you select **View, All Headers**.

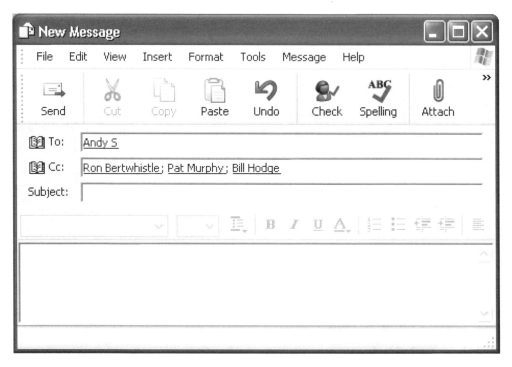

◉   Type in a subject line and a message.

Formatting a message

You can use the buttons on the **Formatting** toolbar to make text bold, underlined, etc. Notice the formatting options are grayed out until you click in the message area. As soon as you've entered the message you can try them out.

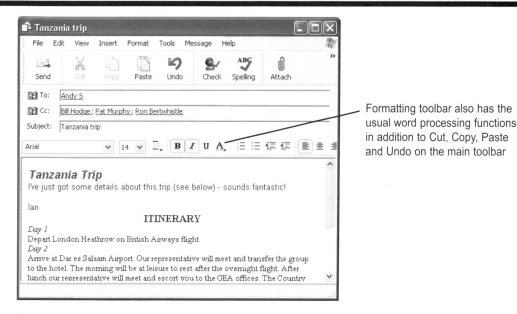

Formatting toolbar also has the usual word processing functions in addition to Cut, Copy, Paste and Undo on the main toolbar

○ Type in 2 or 3 lines, then try moving, deleting, copying and pasting words.

Tip:
You can move selected text within a message by clicking and dragging, just as in Word. Text can also be copied between any messages you have open, using **Cut**, **Copy** and **Paste** on the Formatting toolbar or the **Edit** menu.

○ Now try opening a Word document (such as **Itinerary.doc** on the web site **www.payne-gallway.co.uk**), select and copy some paragraphs and paste them into your e-mail message.

The spell-checking tool finds and corrects both spelling mistakes and repeated words. For example, if you had the text:

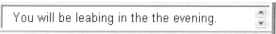

○ Click the **Spelling** button to find the first mistake '**leabing**'.

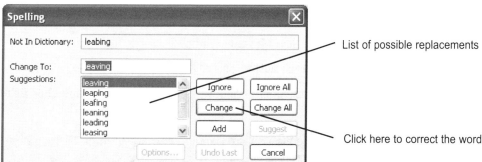

List of possible replacements

Click here to correct the word

○ Click **Change** to replace the misspelt word with the first option and look for the next mistake.

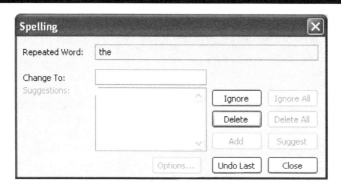

○ Click **Delete** to remove the repeated word 'the'.

Tip:
Although you can format your message using **Outlook Express**, not all recipients will see the formatting if their e-mails are text only or they use some other e-mail programs. It is better to send messages as text only.

If the message is urgent you can indicate this by clicking the **Priority** button arrow and selecting **High Priority** (or **Message**, **Set Priority**, **High**). The message won't get there any sooner but it will stand out.

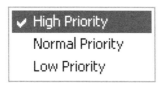

It is important that the Subject field should be accurate and the message spell-checked and not too long. This is called **Network etiquette** or **netiquette**. When the message is ready click **Send** to move it to the Outbox.

Attaching a file

As well as text you can also **attach** one or more files to a message. Each could be a word-processed document, spreadsheet, graphics file, etc.

○ Create a new message and enter address, subject and some text.

To attach a file in the **New Message** window:

○ Click on the **Attach** button on the toolbar.

○ In the Insert **Attachment** window, navigate to the file and click **Attach**.

Tip:
If the total size of the file you are sending is more than half a megabyte (500Kb) then you should compress or **zip** it if you or the receiver have a dial-up connection. (It takes about 5 minutes to send 1Mb of data using a fast modem.) Compressing is described in Module 2 .

Click here to go to the next folder up

Recipe.doc is being attached

The file is now listed in the **Attach** box in the message header.

Tip:
If you change your mind, select the file in the **Attach** box and press **Delete.**

Your message is now complete and ready to send. When you send the message, any attached files go too.

Mailing to a distribution list

If you send regular e-mails to a large group – say a newsletter – you can make a **Group** in the Address book and select its members from the address list. Now you just choose the group name as one recipient.

Tip:
When sending a large mailing, each recipient may have half a page of addresses at the start of the message, which probably means having to print another page. To avoid this, send the message To yourself with the other recipients in Bcc.

Exercises

1. Look up **Addressing e-mail messages** in the Help system.

2. Open the Address Book and add 3 new addresses. (If you are in a class they could be other class members.)

3. Create a new mail message with one of the addresses in the To box and the others in Cc and Bcc.

4. Enter **Attached file** as the subject and **Here's the file** as the text.

5. Attach a Word .doc file to the message (preferably no bigger than 200Kb).

6. Give the message a high **Priority**.

7. Click **Send** to send the message to the Outbox. (Do not connect.)

Messaging

Sending messages from the Outbox

You can send a message straight from the **New Message** window but it's much better to send all the messages from the **Outbox** so that in case of trouble they are still there.

Tip:

If anything goes wrong while sending, you could lose the message and have to type it all in again!

Click the **Send/Recv** button on the toolbar.

This sends all the messages in the Outbox and puts any waiting messages in the Inbox. If you have a **Dial-up connection** and are offline, you will be prompted to go online. In this case click **Yes**, then **Connect** at the next prompt. If the **Hang Up When Finished** box is checked, the **Send and Receive All** option disconnects you automatically at the end.

Tip:

Be sure you have disconnected after sending your messages, unless you have other work to do on the Internet. If the Dial-up icon is visible at the bottom right of your screen, right-click it and choose **Disconnect**.

Outlook Express now sends all messages from the **Outbox**, and if there are any messages waiting in your mailbox, it downloads them from the server (a computer belonging to your Internet Service Provider somewhere) to the **Inbox** (somewhere on your hard disk).

Outlook Express can be set to collect e-mails when you start it up although this is usually inconvenient if you have a dial-up connection. To set this, choose **Tools, Options, General** tab and select **Send and receive messages at startup**.

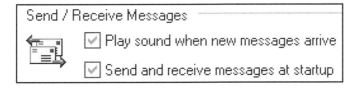

A message may appear telling you what is happening.

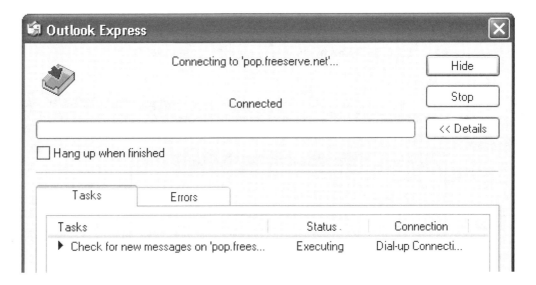

Viewing sent messages

Sometimes it is useful to be able to look up a message you sent last week or last month, to remind yourself what you said. All the messages you send are saved automatically and kept until you delete them.

◗ Click on **Sent Items** in the main window to see what you sent.

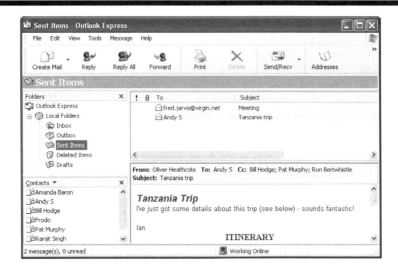

Receiving messages

▶ Click on **Inbox** to show any messages received.

Note:

You may receive unsolicited messages – known as **spam**. These are usually advertising but are sometimes sent just to annoy.

The number in blue shows how many new (unread) messages you have

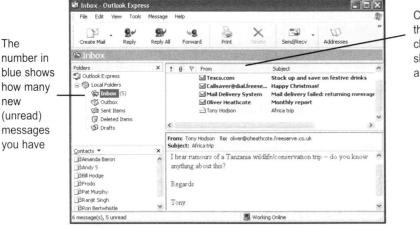

Click here to change the sort order. To change the columns shown, right-click here and choose Columns.

 —— Unread

 —— Read

Tip:

If you select the message title, the content is shown in the pane below.

These are shown on the right with icons indicating **Read** or **Unread**. You can sort the messages by sender, date and so on either by **View, Sort By,** or by clicking the column header. The message is shown in the **Preview** pane below but it is easier to view it in a separate window.

○ Double-click on the message name in the **Message List** pane.

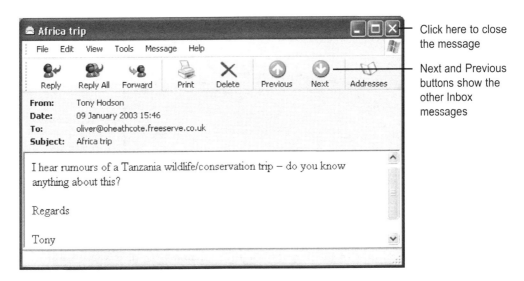

Click here to close the message

Next and Previous buttons show the other Inbox messages

The **Message View** window lets you:

> read and print out the message
>
> type a reply
>
> forward it to someone else
>
> print a message by clicking the **Print** button

You can have 2 or more messages open at once and switch between them using **Alt-Tab**.

Tip:

If you right-click on the sender's name in this window, or on the message in the message list, you can add the sender to the Address Book.

Receiving an attachment

If you receive a file with an attachment, the message header has a paper-clip icon beside it.

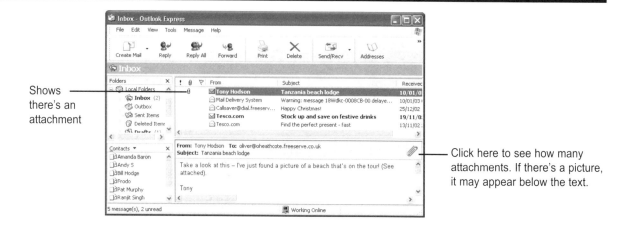

Shows there's an attachment

Click here to see how many attachments. If there's a picture, it may appear below the text.

Saving an attachment

You might want to save an attached file to your hard disk if you want to keep it permanently. Otherwise, when you delete the message you'll delete the attachment too.

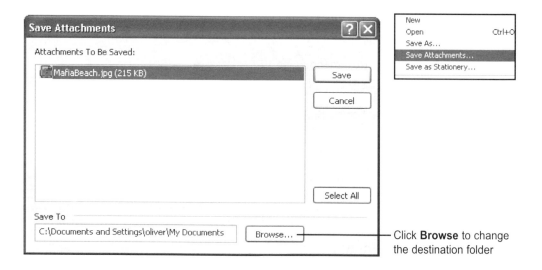

Click **Browse** to change the destination folder

○ Choose **File, Save Attachments**.

The default folder for saving attachments is **Documents and settings\My Documents** but you can change this with the **Browse** button. You can open an attachment without saving it by opening the message and double-clicking on the file name in the Attach box, but first see below concerning viruses.

Virus Alert

Make sure you have an up-to-date virus checker installed. While most file types are safe, it is wise not to open files with .exe, .scr, .pif or .vbs extensions unless you are expecting them.

Opening an unrecognised mail message

There is a risk of infecting a computer with a virus just by opening a message – there's no danger from plain text but if the e-mail is in the form of a web page there may be buttons having unseen effects. You can delete a suspicious-looking message without opening it by hiding the **Preview** pane first (**View**, **Layout**) then right-clicking on it and choosing **Delete**.

If you don't trust a file attachment, save it first then scan it with the virus checker before opening it. You may not see the file extension since Windows hides them by default: in this case, in Windows Explorer choose **Tools, Folder Options, View** tab, uncheck **Hide file extensions for known file types** then click **Like Current Folder**.

Replying to a message

◉ Click on the **Reply** button on the toolbar.

The reply window is all set up for you to type a reply to the sender only.

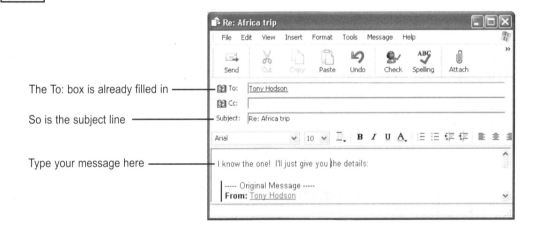

The To: box is already filled in

So is the subject line

Type your message here

Reply All sends a reply to anyone else that that message was sent to.

◉ Type your message and click **Send**.

The reply should normally be kept brief. The original message is normally included in the reply as a reminder. If you don't want this (perhaps if the original message was very long), choose **Tools, Options** and on the **Send** tab, uncheck **Include message in reply**.

☑ Include message in reply

It should be put in the Outbox.

Tip:
We have set Outlook Express to send all messages to the Outbox.

Forwarding a message

A message sent to you might be of interest to someone else too. Try forwarding a message.

◗ Double-click on the message name in the **Inbox** to show the message view window.

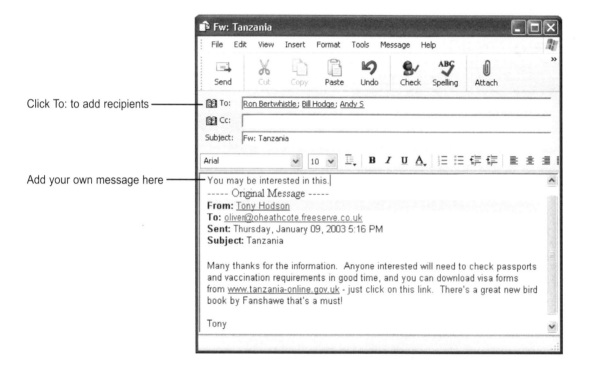

◗ Click on the **Forward** button.

The forwarding window is all set up, with a subject line of **Fw: [your message title]**. The cursor is in the message area with the forwarding message below.

◗ Click **To:** to add the recipient's name.

Click To: to add recipients ——

Add your own message here ——

◗ Add your own message if you like and click **Send**.

Signatures

You may like to add a standard ending to some messages without having to type it all in every time. To do this, go to **Tools**, **Options**, **Signature** and enter the text – or even a scanned image of your signature! You then call it up in the New Message window with **Insert**, **Signature**.

Digital signature

As e-mail becomes increasingly used to send confidential information, it is important to be sure that e-mailed documents are not intercepted and can be read only by the intended recipient(s). To send a secure e-mail you must obtain a digital ID from a certification authority (see Outlook Express Help). Then, from the New message window choose **Tools**, **Digitally Sign** and a digital ID is added which matches your e-mail address. To encrypt the message as well choose **Tools**, **Encrypt**. Reading a digitally signed e-mail is as for a normal message, but there is a security warning if it has been tampered with. You can read an encrypted message from a contact once you have sent them a digitally signed message.

A digital ID consists of a public key, private key and a digital signature. Digitally signing a message adds your digital signature and a public key, together comprising a certificate. To read an encrypted message requires your private key.

Exercises

1. Open Outlook Express.

2. Get someone to send you an e-mail with an attachment.

3. Click **Send/Recv** to collect e-mail for your address.

4. View the message in the Preview pane.

5. Double-click on the header to view the message in a new window.

6. Send a reply to the message.

7. Forward the message to another address.

Mail Management

Once you have sent and received quite a few messages, they start to build up in the **InBox** and **Sent Items** so that you have to scroll a long way to find a message. You need to **sort** the messages, **delete** those you don't need and **file** those you do.

Sorting messages

You can sort the messages in a folder by sender, subject or date, by clicking the column header (clicking again reverses the order).

Priority, Attachment and Flag —

!	0	▽	From	Subject	Received
			Mail Delivery System	Warning: message 18Wdkc-0008CB-00 delaye...	10/01/03 04:49
		▼	Tony Hodson	Tanzania	09/01/03 17:15
			Tony Hodson	Africa trip	09/01/03 15:52
			Oliver Heathcote	Monthly report	09/01/03 15:18
			Mail Delivery System	Mail delivery failed: returning message to sender	09/01/03 14:33
			Callsaver@dial.freeserv...	Happy Christmas!	25/12/02 11:02
			Tesco.com	**Stock up and save on festive drinks**	**19/11/02 20:46**
			Tesco.com	Find the perfect present - fast	13/11/02 21:42

In the left-hand columns, the **Priority** shows if a priority level was set by the sender. **Attachments** (the paper clip) are discussed in the next chapter. Clicking in the Flag column shows a **Flag** icon to draw your attention. (Click again to remove it.) You can sort on these 3 columns as well. The Read/Unread markers can be changed from the **Edit** menu.

Searching for messages

With large numbers of messages it is useful to search for matching messages.

◉   Click the **Find** button, enter search parameters and click **Find Now**.

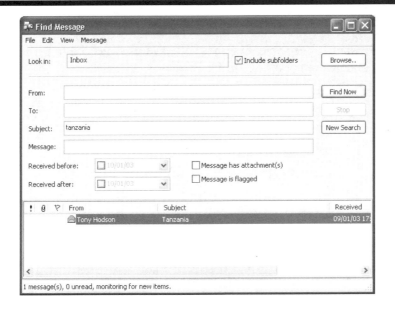

Tip:
Search on sender, recipient, subject, content or date range.

Selecting from a list

Rather than do this message by message, it's much quicker to select several at once in a list, and then either delete or file them. Suppose you want to select five messages in the **Inbox** list. If these are all together:

◉ Select the first, then hold down **Shift** and click on the last.

If the messages are not together:

◉ Select the first, then hold down **Ctrl** and click on each. Notice that this is a **toggle**: if you **Ctrl-click** on a selected message, it deselects it.

Deleting messages

It's best to be ruthless and delete any message you don't need to keep. This includes nearly everything in **Sent Items**. To delete messages:

◉ Select the messages in the **Sent Items** folder and click the **Delete** button.

This moves them to the **Deleted Items** folder so they are not actually lost. When this folder starts to fill up, choose **Edit**, **Empty 'Deleted Items' folder**. Alternatively to delete them automatically choose **Tools**, **Options**, **Maintenance** tab, and check **Empty messages from the 'Deleted Items' folder on exit**.

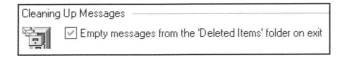

Organising messages

You'll probably want to file some messages you have received in a folder for easy identification and delete the others. To file messages:

○ Select the messages in the main window.

Tip:

Use **Ctrl-click**

○ From the **Edit** menu, choose **Move to Folder**.

Tip:
You can also drag a message between folders but not into the Outbox. Recover a deleted message from Deleted Items.

The **Move** window shows all the **Local Folders** you see in the Inbox. You need to make a new folder.

○ Click the **New Folder** button and type a name for the folder, such as **Personal**.

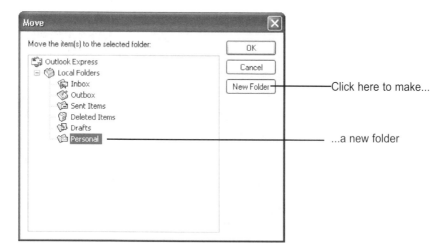

Click here to make...

...a new folder

○ Click **OK**, then **OK** again to move the messages from the Inbox to your new folder.

If you get interrupted in the middle of writing a long e-mail and aren't sure when you can continue, just click **Send** (don't connect) to put it in the Outbox, then move it to the **Drafts** folder. You can then finish it at leisure and click **Send** to move it to the Outbox. Closing Outlook Express while a message is incomplete automatically puts it in Drafts.

Printing a message

You can print a message from most windows by clicking the **Print** button or **File, Print**. Look at it in the Preview window first – if it's long you may want to just select a part of it for printing.

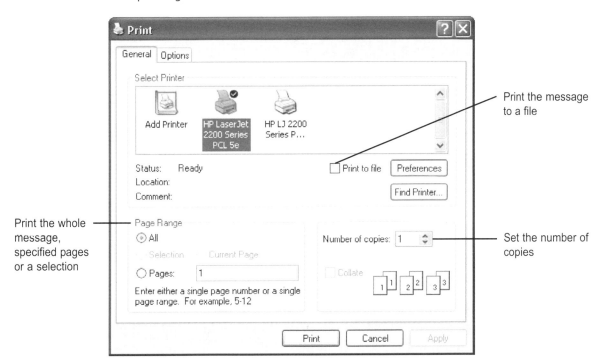

Print the whole message, specified pages or a selection

Print the message to a file

Set the number of copies

Closing Outlook Express

 ◗ Select **File, Close** or click the **X** icon on the title bar.

 ◗ If the **Dial-up** icon is still shown in the Status bar, right-click it and choose **Disconnect**.

Exercises

1. Open Outlook Express. For this exercise, you need at least 6 messages in the Inbox.

2. Delete a message and view it in the **Deleted Items** folder.

3. Empty the **Deleted Items** folder.

4. Sort the messages by sender, then content, then date received.

5. Mark a read message as unread.

6. Create a new folder and name it **Special**.

7. Select 3 messages together and move them into the new folder.

8. Mark one message with a flag.

Index — Information and Communication

juiced
squeezed + shaken

Published by Murdoch Books®, a division of Murdoch Magazines Pty Ltd.

Murdoch Books® Australia
Pier 8/9, 23 Hickson Road
Miller's Point NSW 2000
Phone: +61 (0) 2 4352 7000
Fax: +61 (0) 2 4352 7026

Murdoch Books UK Limited
Erico House
6th Floor North
93–99 Upper Richmond Road
Putney, London SW15 2TG
Phone: +44 (0) 20 8785 5995
Fax: +44 (0) 20 8785 5985

Design Concept: Marylouise Brammer
Designer: Tracy Loughlin
Editorial Director: Diana Hill
Additional Text: Francesca Newby
Project Manager: Zoë Harpham
Editor: Stephanie Kistner
Recipes developed and tested by Jane Lawson and the Murdoch Books Test Kitchen team.
Production: Monika Vidovic

Chief Executive: Juliet Rogers
Publisher: Kay Scarlett

National Library of Australia Cataloguing-in-Publication Data
Juiced. Includes index. ISBN 1 74045 229 1
1. Beverages. 641.2

PRINTED IN CHINA by Toppan Printing Co. (HK) Ltd.
Printed 2004.

IMPORTANT: Those who might be at risk from the effects of salrnonella food poisoning (the elderly, pregnant
women, young children and those suffering from immune deficiency diseases) should consult their doctor with
any concerns about eating raw eggs.

juiced
squeezed + shaken

MURDOCH BOOKS

contents

getting juiced

When life has squeezed you dry or left you shaken and stirred there is a place you can turn to for sustenance. Whether it's your body or soul that needs restoring, look to your kitchen. All you need is some fruit and a little inspiration and you'll have a whole lot of healing going on.

There's nothing magic about it, no charms are needed to harness the essential goodness of fresh ripe fruit, vegies, milk, soy and grains. Juicing is simply the easiest way to ensure you get the recommended levels of vitamins and minerals, without boring yourself to death. Completing your diet by creating your own drinks is not just delicious, it's a smart thing to do. Short of munching them raw the moment they're taken from the tree or pulled from the ground, there is no more efficient way to extract the nutrients that we need.

Knowing what to do and how to do it is the key to juicing, and the basics live up to their name. There is some equipment and a little know-how involved, but nothing that can't be mastered easily or isn't worth the effort.

Fruit

Using fruit that is fresh and ripe is the one essential, both for taste and nourishment. Seasonality is another factor — strawberries taste best when warmed in the sun and apples are crisp in autumn for a reason.

A comprehensive list of fruiting seasons would take a bigger tome than this but the basics are fairly instinctive.

Summer: Tropical fruits, soft stone fruits, berries, cherries, melons and grapes.

Autumn: Orchard fruits like apples and pears are ripe for the picking; the last berries come through.

Winter: Oranges rule in the warmer climates.

Spring: Leading into summer, tropical fruits, melons and passionfruit begin to appear.

Bananas bless us all year round.

Get to know your grocer or make the markets a habit to get a sense of what you want and when it's available. Supplement the leaner months with high-quality dried and frozen fruit. Stone fruits dry particularly well and berries freeze brilliantly. Fruit tinned in its own juice also makes the grade.

equipment

Assuming your kitchen isn't bristling with gadgets, you may need to buy a few extra bits and bobs. An excellent excuse to go shopping, and you can go all out or start as simply as you like.

The first thing you'll need is a citrus juicer. A cheap pyrex squeezer will do the job, as will the iconic Philippe Starck tripod or a citrus press with a lever arm. Limes and lemons are best attacked with a chunky wooden reamer.

A juicer is a must if you're going to be serious about this. You don't need the most expensive version, just one that suits your needs. Whichever model you choose, remember 'easy-to-clean' is not an optional extra.

Blenders are essential for good smoothies. A robust, professional model will crush ice and last forever and the price will reflect this. If you want to start cheaply get a hand-held number and crush ice by smashing it in a plastic bag with a rolling pin.

Anything else you need will probably be found lurking in the second drawer down. A knife, a vegetable peeler, a strainer and the above-mentioned rolling pin should see you through the most complicated recipe.

Fruit + vegie juices.
Juices are as varied as the fruit, vegetables and herbs we use to make them. Packed with vitamins and minerals, fresh juices should be consumed as quickly as possible before oxidization causes the essential nutrients to deteriorate.

Sparklies + fizzes.
Light and bubbly, these are the drinks to serve with food. Diluting juices with soft drink or soda means the flavours of the food get the starring role.

Frappés + freezies.
Crystalline and icy, frappés and freezies use crushed ice to add body. You can serve them as dessert, or just to freshen up a hot afternoon.

Shakes + smoothies.
Thick and lush, smoothies and shakes can be an indulgent treat or a meal in a glass. As a rule of thumb, a shake is made with ice cream and a smoothie is based on yoghurt.

Teas + tonics.
Prepared with tea and fresh herbs as well as fruits and syrups, teas and tonics make great remedies. If you have a cold to shift or an ache to relieve, this is the chapter to turn to. The fact that they taste terrific is just a bonus!

fruit + vegie juices

Put on some Barry White, slip into a long cool stretch of black velvet and get in the mood for some lurve.

black velvet

500 g (1 lb 2 oz) black seedless grapes
300 g (10^1/$_2$ oz) blackberries
400 g (2 cups) cherries, pitted
ice cubes, to serve

Juice the grapes, blackberries and cherries through a juice extractor. Stir to combine and serve over ice. Makes 2 small glasses.

Note: This juice is very rich and sweet so only makes a small amount. You can top it up with soda water to make 4 tall glasses.

Be a killer queen with this potent concoction and shoot down those germs in style.

cold killer

4 celery stalks
1 kg (2 lb 4 oz) carrots
2 garlic cloves
10 g (^{1}/2 cup) flat-leaf (Italian) parsley
2 teaspoons honey

Juice the celery, carrots, garlic and parsley through a juice extractor. Stir through the honey. Makes 2 medium glasses.

Been living on the wild side? Give your kidneys a chance to regroup with this healing drink.

kidney cleanser

800 g (4 cups) chopped watermelon
1 large cucumber
3 apples, stalks removed
250 ml (1 cup) cranberry juice

Juice the watermelon, cucumber and apples through a juice extractor. Stir through the cranberry juice. Makes 2 large glasses.

Even the meanest machine needs the occasional tune-up.

green machine

6 celery stalks
2 apples, stalks removed
125 g (4 1/2 oz) alfalfa sprouts
10 g (1/2 cup) flat-leaf (Italian) parsley
10 g (1/2 cup) mint leaves

Juice the celery, apples, alfalfa sprouts, parsley and mint through a juice extractor. Stir to combine. Makes 2 medium glasses.

A classic Italian soup is transformed into this spicy drink.

gazpacho in a glass

6 vine-ripened tomatoes
1 red capsicum (pepper)
1 lemon, peeled
2 large cucumbers
10 g ($1/2$ cup) parsley
1 garlic clove
dash of Tabasco
ice cubes, to serve
extra virgin olive oil, to serve, optional

Juice the tomatoes, capsicum, lemon, cucumbers, parsley and garlic through a juice extractor. Stir through the Tabasco, to taste. Serve over ice with a drizzle of extra virgin olive oil, if desired. Makes 2 large glasses.

Enhance your cool factor with a chilled shot of cucumber.

cool as a cucumber

3 large cucumbers
3 limes, peeled
20 g (1 cup) mint leaves
1 1/2 tablespoons caster (superfine) sugar

Juice the cucumbers, limes and mint through a juice extractor. Stir through the sugar. Makes 2 large glasses.

Carrot and lime receive a soothing fragrant lift through the addition of rosewater and cinnamon in this Arabian Nights inspired drink.

carrot, lime and rosewater juice

1.5 kg (3 lb 5 oz) carrots
3 limes, peeled
1 teaspoon rosewater
large pinch ground cinnamon
ice cubes, to serve

Juice the carrots and limes through a juice extractor. Stir through the rosewater and cinnamon and serve over ice. Makes 2 medium glasses.

Instant winter warming with a zing of ginger and a healthy dose of vitamins.

warm carrot and ginger shots

2 kg (4 1b 8 oz) carrots
4 cm (1¹/2 inch) piece ginger
1 tablespoon lemon juice
large pinch ground cinnamon
large pinch ground cumin
natural yoghurt, to serve, optional

Juice the carrots and ginger through a juice extractor. Transfer to a saucepan with the lemon juice, cinnamon and cumin. Stir over medium heat until just warmed through, then pour into shot glasses and top each with a small dollop of yoghurt. Makes 8 shot glasses or 2 large glasses.

Don't be a dill — revive and survive with this smart concoction.

cucumber, apple and dill juice

2 large cucumbers
9 apples, stalks removed
2 tablespoons dill
1 lemon, peeled
ice cubes, to serve

Juice the cucumbers, apples, dill and lemon through a juice extractor. Stir to combine and serve over ice. Makes 2 medium glasses.

A shot of this green magic will get you through a grey day.

apple, celery, cucumber and basil juice

9 apples, stalks removed
6 celery stalks
1 large cucumber
7 g (1/4 cup) basil leaves

Juice the apples, celery, cucumber and basil through a juice extractor. Stir to combine. Makes 2 large glasses.

Don't just grapple with a cold, tackle it to the ground with zucchini, full of vitamin C and antioxidants.

zapple

6 apples, stalks removed
2 zucchini (courgettes)
3 cm (1¼ inch) piece ginger
ice cubes, to serve

Juice the apples, zucchini and ginger through a juice extractor. Stir to combine and serve over ice. Makes 2 large glasses.

This gorgeous juice is subtle and simple.

blushing nashi zinger

6 Nashi pears, stalks removed
250 g (9 oz) strawberries, hulled
3 cm (1¼ inch) piece ginger

Juice the pears, strawberries and ginger through a juice extractor. Stir to combine. Makes 2 large glasses.

Note: Use pears that are ripe, but not overripe, otherwise they won't juice well.

This bird won't give you wings but it will help elevate your immune system.

strange bird

500 g (1 lb 2 oz) strawberries, hulled
6 kiwifruit, peeled
ice cubes, to serve

Juice the strawberries and kiwifruit through a juice extractor. Stir to combine and serve over ice. Makes 2 small glasses.

An excellent antioxidant. Turn to this drink when you've been hitting the other grape juice a little too hard.

kiwi, grape and orange juice

6 kiwifruit, peeled
500 g (1 lb 2 oz) green seedless grapes
3 oranges, peeled
1 large passionfruit, halved

Juice the kiwifruit, grapes and oranges through a juice extractor. Scoop out the passionfruit pulp and stir through the juice. Makes 2 large glasses.

The mild green goodness of kiwifruit gently undercuts the acid kick of pineapple.

pineapple, kiwi and mint

1/2 small pineapple, peeled and chopped
6 kiwifruit, peeled
10 g (1/2 cup) mint leaves
2 cm (3/4 inch) piece ginger

Juice the pineapple, kiwifruit, mint and ginger through a juice extractor. Stir to combine. Makes 2 medium glasses.

Invest in some star appeal at breakfast and you'll be shining all day long.

star appeal

6 kiwifruit, peeled
4 starfruit (carambola)
1 small pineapple, peeled and chopped

Juice the kiwifruit, starfruit and pineapple through a juice extractor. Stir to combine. Makes 2 large glasses.

The sweetest and gentlest of the melons, honeydew is the perfect companion to tart and tangy lemon juice.

kiwi, honeydew and lemon juice

6 kiwifruit, peeled
1 honeydew melon, peeled, seeded and chopped
1 lemon, peeled

Juice the kiwifruit, honeydew and lemon through a juice extractor. Stir to combine. Makes 2 medium glasses.

Life's a bowl of cherries so juice them up and forget about the pits.

cherry, black grape and apple juice

400 g (2 cups) cherries, pitted
500 g (1 lb 2 oz) black or green
seedless grapes
6 apples, stalks removed
250 ml (1 cup) cranberry juice
ice cubes, to serve

Juice the cherries, grapes and apples through a juice extractor. Stir through the cranberry juice and serve over ice. Makes 2 large glasses.

Jazz up this gentle duo with a full-on blast of ginger spice.

apple, celery and ginger juice

9 apples, stalks removed
9 celery stalks
3 cm (1¼ inch) piece ginger

Juice the apples, celery and ginger through a juice extractor. Stir to combine. Makes 2 large glasses.

Gorgeously green with a minty zing, this drink captures a fresh spring morning in a glass.

honeydew, pineapple and mint juice

1 honeydew melon, peeled, seeded and chopped
1 small pineapple, peeled and chopped
10 g (1/2 cup) mint leaves

Juice the honeydew, pineapple and mint through a juice extractor. Stir to combine. Makes 2 large glasses.

If in need of a little get up and go, grab this: the melons provide natural sweetness while the ginger brings its unique sharp zap to the mix.

gingered melon juice

1 honeydew melon, peeled, seeded and chopped
1 rockmelon (netted/US cantaloupe), peeled, seeded and chopped
2 cm (3/4 inch) piece ginger

Juice the honeydew, rockmelon and ginger through a juice extractor. Stir to combine. Makes 2 medium glasses.

For a sunrise special, juice the strawberries separately then stir them through in a loose crimson swirl.

papaya, rockmelon and strawberry juice

1 papaya, peeled and seeded
1 rockmelon (netted/US cantaloupe), peeled, seeded and chopped
500 g (1 lb 2 oz) strawberries, hulled
2 limes, peeled
ice cubes, to serve

Juice the papaya, rockmelon, strawberries and limes through a juice extractor. Stir to combine and serve over ice. Makes 2 medium glasses.

When you're melting under the summer sun, reverse the trend with this cool concoction.

zippy grape and apple juice

500 g (1 lb 2 oz) green seedless grapes
6 apples, stalks removed
1 lemon, peeled
ice cubes, to serve

Juice the grapes, apples and lemon through a juice extractor. Stir to combine and serve over ice. Makes 2 medium glasses.

Note: Freeze the juice in ice-block trays for a refreshing treat.

As green as the hills, as gold as the sun — surely a natural choice.

green and gold

250 g (9 oz) green seedless grapes
6 oranges, peeled
2 lemons, peeled
1 teaspoon honey

Juice the grapes, oranges and lemons through a juice extractor. Stir through the honey. Makes 2 large glasses.

Pretty in pink with an acid twist — there's nothing sugary about this tart cooler.

pink grapefruit, mint and cranberry juice

2 pink grapefruit
500 ml (2 cups) cranberry juice
2 tablespoons finely chopped mint leaves
ice cubes, to serve

Squeeze the juice from the grapefruit. Stir through the cranberry juice and mint and serve over ice. Makes 2 large glasses.

With vitamin C-rich guava, this little baby will have you back in the pink.

think pink

3 pink grapefruit, peeled
250 g (9 oz) strawberries, hulled
375 ml (1½ cups) guava juice
ice cubes, to serve

Juice the grapefruit and strawberries through a juice extractor. Stir through the guava juice and serve over ice. Makes 2 large glasses.

Butterflies can flutter at any time. Soothe them away with this calming tonic.

tummy calmer

50 g (2 cups) English spinach leaves
400 g (14 oz) cabbage
4 apples, stalks removed

Juice the spinach, cabbage and apples through a juice extractor. Stir to combine. Makes 2 small glasses.

Life can be a marathon and a sprint, so when you need a fuel injection, reach for your juicer.

spinach energizer

50 g (2 cups) baby English spinach leaves
1 large cucumber
3 apples, stalks removed
3 celery stalks
1 baby fennel
10 g (1/2 cup) parsley

Juice the spinach, cucumber, apples, celery, fennel and parsley through a juice extractor. Stir to combine. Makes 2 large glasses.

Feeling seedy? This thick, luscious juice calms the inner storm.

mango, apple and lime juice

3 mangoes, peeled and stones removed
6 apples, stalks removed
2 limes, peeled
2 cm (3/4 inch) piece ginger
honey, to taste, optional

Juice the mangoes, apples, limes and ginger through a juice extractor. Stir through a little honey, if desired. Makes 2 medium glasses.

Serve this divine juice with a frangipani peeking coyly over the edge.

orange tropical blossom

4 oranges
1 mango, peeled, stone removed and chopped
1/2 small papaya, peeled, seeded and chopped
1 1/2 teaspoons orange flower water
ice cubes, to serve

Juice the oranges in a citrus press. Blend the orange juice, mango, papaya and orange flower water in a blender until smooth. Serve over ice. Makes 2 medium glasses.

Play it again, Sam. Evoke the romance of Casablanca with this fragrant, exotic juice.

orange blossom citrus refresher

6 oranges, peeled
20 g (1 cup) mint leaves
1 1/2 teaspoons orange flower water
1 teaspoon pomegranate syrup
ice cubes, to serve
mint sprigs, to garnish
pomegranate syrup, extra, to serve, optional

Juice the oranges and mint through a juice extractor. Stir through the orange flower water and pomegranate syrup and serve over ice, garnished with mint. Drizzle over a little more pomegranate syrup, if desired. Makes 2 medium glasses.

Honey and vanilla coax out the natural sweetness of the humble carrot.

carrot, orange and cardamom juice

1 kg (2 lb 4 oz) carrots
6 oranges, peeled
small pinch of ground cardamom
1 teaspoon natural vanilla extract (essence)
1 teaspoon honey
ice cubes, to serve

Juice the carrots and oranges through a juice extractor. Stir through the cardamom, vanilla and honey, and serve over ice. Makes 2 large glasses.

If orange juice doesn't do it for you anymore, give this a go.

plum, orange and vanilla nectar

10 small plums, stones removed
6 oranges, peeled
1/2 teaspoon natural vanilla extract (essence)
ice cubes, to serve

Juice the plums and oranges through a juice extractor. Stir through the vanilla and serve over ice. Makes 2 large glasses.

Note: Use the ripest plums you can find.

Mix cherries with berries for a sensory overload and leave it up to the apples to add a note of calm.

berries and cherries

150 g (5 1/2 oz) blueberries
200 g (1 cup) cherries, pitted
6 apples, stalks removed
ice cubes, to serve

Juice the blueberries, cherries and apples through a juice extractor. Stir to combine and serve over ice. Makes 2 medium glasses.

Tender young fennel bulbs add a fresh, astringent liquorice kick to good old apple and orange juice.

fennel, apple and orange juice

1 baby fennel
3 apples, stalks removed
6 oranges, peeled
7 g (¼ cup) basil leaves
1 teaspoon honey, optional

Juice the fennel, apples, oranges and basil through a juice extractor. Stir through the honey, if desired. Makes 2 large glasses.

Pungent basil leaves bring out the delicate sweetness of fresh ripe nectarines.

nectarine and basil juice

4 nectarines, stones removed
15 g (1/2 cup) basil leaves
4 oranges, peeled

Juice the nectarines, basil and oranges through a juice extractor. Stir to combine. Makes 2 medium glasses.

Vamp it up with ruby red blood oranges.

fennel, blood orange and cranberry juice

1 baby fennel
375 ml (1¹/2 cups) blood orange juice
375 ml (1¹/2 cups) cranberry juice
ice cubes, to serve

Juice the baby fennel through a juice extractor. Stir through the blood orange juice and cranberry juice and serve over ice. Makes 2 large glasses.

Sweet yet light, this is the perfect juice for a particularly delicate morning.

grapefruit, pear and guava sunrise

2 grapefruit, peeled
4 pears, stalks removed
375 ml (1 1/2 cups) guava juice
ice cubes, to serve

Juice the grapefruit and pears through a juice extractor. Stir through the guava juice and serve over ice. Makes 2 large glasses.

Take the sting out of an early start with this totally citrus antidote.

citrus sting

2 limes
3 grapefruit
6 oranges
honey, to taste

Juice the limes, grapefruit and oranges in a citrus press. Stir through the honey. Makes 4 large glasses.

Good things begin with g — gemstones, girls and grape'n'guava.

grape'n'guava

500 g (1 lb 2 oz) green or black
seedless grapes
2 cm (3/4 inch) piece ginger
1 lime, peeled
4 large passionfruit, halved
375 ml (1 1/2 cups) guava juice
ice cubes, to serve

Juice the grapes, ginger and lime through a juice extractor. Strain the passionfruit pulp, discarding the seeds. Combine the passionfruit juice with the grape mixture and guava juice. Serve over ice. Makes 2 medium glasses.

Some days you need quiet, calming, gentle drinks. Other days you don't.

sweet and spicy plum

10 small plums, stones removed
3 cm (1¼ inch) piece ginger
200 g (1 cup) cherries, pitted
3 oranges, peeled
20 g (1 cup) mint leaves
1 teaspoon honey
ice cubes, to serve

Juice the plums, ginger, cherries, oranges and mint through a juice extractor. Stir through the honey and serve over ice. Makes 2 medium glasses.

Everyone knows apricots look like cute little bottoms. They're also ridiculously good for you. Grab them while you can.

apricot, orange and ginger juice

10 apricots, stones removed
6 oranges, peeled
3 cm (1¹/4 inch) piece ginger
ice cubes, to serve

Juice the apricots, oranges and ginger through a juice extractor. Stir to combine and serve over ice. Makes 2 large glasses.

Sweet and exotic, this juice is perfect for a languid afternoon tea.

turkish delight

2–3 lemons, to taste	Juice the lemons in a citrus press.
1 teaspoon rosewater	Stir through the rosewater, honey and
2 teaspoons honey	375 ml (1$1/2$ cups) cold water. Serve over ice.
ice cubes, to serve	Makes 2 large glasses.

Apple, berry, cherry … let's start at the very beginning, a very good place to start!

abc

6 apples, stalks removed
150 g (5 1/2 oz) raspberries
400 g (2 cups) cherries, pitted
ice cubes, to serve

Juice the apples, raspberries and cherries through a juice extractor. Stir to combine and serve over ice. Makes 2 large glasses.

Burst onto the scene with this feel-good golden blast.

pine lime burst

1 pineapple, peeled and chopped
2 limes, peeled
500 g (1 lb 2 oz) strawberries, hulled

Juice the pineapple, limes and strawberries through a juice extractor. Stir to combine. Makes 2 medium glasses.

The sweetest member of the rose family, a fresh peach brings a flush of unadulterated good health to the cheeks.

peach, kiwi and apple juice

4 peaches, stones removed
6 kiwifruit, peeled
3 apples, stalks removed

Juice the peaches, kiwifruit and apples through a juice extractor. Stir to combine. Makes 2 large glasses.

Strong and spicy, line up the shot glasses and find out who's really the tough guy.

red ginger

10 small plums, stones removed
500 g (1 lb 2 oz) red seedless grapes
2 limes, peeled
3 cm (1¼ inch) piece ginger
10 g (½ cup) mint leaves
ice cubes, to serve

Juice the plums, grapes, limes, ginger and mint through a juice extractor. Stir to combine and serve over ice. Makes 4 shot glasses.

An extravaganza of succulent stone fruit, tempered with the refreshing tang of oranges.

summer orange

3 oranges, peeled
5 small plums, stones removed
4 peaches, stones removed
10 apricots, stones removed

Juice the oranges, plums, peaches and apricots through a juice extractor. Stir to combine. Makes 2 large glasses.

A sweet combination that's picture perfect for a couple of sweethearts to share.

nectarine, grape and strawberry juice

6 nectarines, stones removed
500 g (1 lb 2 oz) green grapes
250 g (9 oz) strawberries, hulled
ice cubes, to serve

Juice the nectarines, grapes and strawberries through a juice extractor. Stir to combine and serve over ice. Makes 2 large glasses.

The ultimate thirst quencher, watermelon makes a satisfying base for this piquant cooler.

watermelon, grape and peach juice

800 g (4 cups) chopped watermelon
500 g (1 lb 2 oz) green or red seedless grapes
4 peaches, stones removed
2 large passionfruit, halved

Juice the watermelon, grapes and peaches through a juice extractor. Scoop out the passionfruit pulp and stir through the juice. Makes 2 large glasses.

Make this in the mellow months of autumn, when the orchards are heavy with sun-ripened fruit.

minted apple orchard

6 apples, stalks removed	Juice the apples, pears and mint through
3 pears, stalks removed	a juice extractor. Stir to combine.
20 g (1 cup) mint leaves	Makes 2 large glasses.

Go ape for the grape and get some seriously potent antioxidant action.

grape ape!

500 g (1 lb 2 oz) red grapes
10 apricots, stones removed
4 pears, stalks removed
3 apples, stalks removed

Juice the grapes, apricots, pears and apples through a juice extractor. Stir to combine. Makes 2 large glasses.

When the spirit is willing but the body a little sluggish, let vitamin-rich melon and naturally sweet grapes give you the boost you need.

red grape and rockmelon juice

500 g (1 lb 2 oz) red seedless grapes
1 rockmelon (netted/US cantaloupe), peeled, seeded and chopped
2 cm (3/4 inch) piece ginger

Juice the grapes, rockmelon and ginger through a juice extractor. Stir to combine. Makes 2 medium glasses.

Transport yourself to Sicily, the home of the best blood oranges, with this deeply flavoursome juice.

blood orange fruit burst

250 g (9 oz) strawberries, hulled
10 apricots, stones removed
250 g (9 oz) lychees, peeled and seeded
375 ml (1½ cups) blood orange juice
ice cubes, to serve

Juice the strawberries, apricots and lychees through a juice extractor. Stir through the blood orange juice and serve over ice. Makes 2 large glasses.

This smooth, thick drink has style and substance — it can't help but be good for you.

tropical slurp

1 small pineapple, peeled and chopped
3 oranges, peeled
1 large banana, chopped
1 mango, peeled, stone removed and chopped
ice cubes, to serve

Juice the pineapple and oranges through a juice extractor. Transfer to a blender with the banana and mango and blend until smooth. Serve over ice. Makes 2 medium glasses.

Even endless summers drift to a close — help them linger with this long, slow cooler.

watermelon and kiwi cooler

1.2 kg (6 cups) chopped watermelon
6 kiwifruit, peeled
ice cubes, to serve

Juice the watermelon and kiwifruit through a juice extractor. Stir to combine and serve over ice. Makes 2 medium glasses.

This drink fixes you up all squeaky-clean on the inside — shame it's not a toner too.

watermelon and guava cleanser

800 g (4 cups) chopped watermelon
3 cm (1 1/4 inch) piece ginger
7 g (1/3 cup) mint leaves
500 ml (2 cups) guava juice
ice cubes, to serve

Juice the watermelon, ginger and mint through a juice extractor. Stir through the guava juice and serve over ice. Makes 2 large glasses.

I can see clearly now my juicer's here.

honeyed carrots

1 kg (2 lb 4 oz) carrots
125 g (4 1/2 oz) alfalfa sprouts
4 pears, stalks removed
1–2 teaspoons honey, to taste

Juice the carrots, alfalfa and pears through a juice extractor. Stir through the honey. Makes 2 medium glasses.

Ramp up the passion factor with a zinger of a juice — serve just before bed!

strawberry, rockmelon and passionfruit juice

500 g (1 lb 2 oz) strawberries, hulled
1 small rockmelon (netted/US cantaloupe), peeled, seeded and chopped
2 large passionfruit, halved

Juice the strawberries and rockmelon through a juice extractor. Scoop out the passionfruit pulp and stir through the juice. Makes 2 medium glasses.

Baby carrots are the sweetest of the bunch, their gentle fronds a sure sign of freshness.

carrot, apricot and nectarine delight

1 kg (2 lb 4 oz) baby carrots
10 apricots, stones removed
4 large nectarines, stones removed
ice cubes, to serve
lemon slices, to serve

Juice the carrots, apricots and nectarines through a juice extractor. Stir to combine and serve over ice with lemon slices. Makes 2 large glasses.

Let exquisitely perfumed lychees clear out a fuzzy morning head.

perfumed nectarine

6 large nectarines, stones removed	Juice the nectarines, peaches and lychees
4 peaches, stones removed	through a juice extractor. Stir to combine.
250 g (9 oz) lychees, peeled and seeded	Makes 2 large glasses.

On those occasions when the body isn't the temple it should be, give it a boost with iron-rich tomato.

carrot, tomato, lemon and basil juice

1 kg (2 lb 4 oz) carrots
4 vine-ripened tomatoes
1 lemon, peeled
10 g (1/3 cup) basil leaves

Juice the carrots, tomatoes, lemon and basil through a juice extractor. Stir to combine. Makes 2 medium glasses.

A froufrou fancy for a girly afternoon.

pink pom pom

4 pink grapefruit, peeled
500 g (1 lb 2 oz) black seedless grapes
3 large passionfruit, halved
1 teaspoon pomegranate syrup
honey, to taste
ice cubes, to serve

Juice the grapefruit and grapes through a juice extractor. Scoop out the passionfruit pulp and stir through the juice, along with the pomegranate syrup and honey. Serve over ice. Makes 2 large glasses.

Drink your way to tropical heaven.

pineapple, pear and guava nectar

1 small pineapple, peeled and chopped
4 pears, stalks removed
250 ml (1 cup) guava juice
ice cubes, to serve

Juice the pineapple and pears through a juice extractor. Stir through the guava juice and serve over ice. Makes 2 large glasses.

Note: For a smoother juice, try cutting out the woody heart of the pineapple.

Like a ruby red stiletto, this is a sharp and sophisticated drop.

raspberry, pear and grape juice

250 g (9 oz) raspberries
4 pears, stalks removed
500 g (1 lb 2 oz) green grapes
ice cubes, to serve

Juice the raspberries, pears and grapes through a juice extractor. Stir to combine and serve over ice. Makes 2 large glasses.

Sometimes only a bit of rough will do.

rough melon

800 g (4 cups) chopped watermelon
1 small pineapple, peeled and chopped
500 g (1 lb 2 oz) green seedless grapes

Juice the watermelon, pineapple and grapes through a juice extractor. Stir to combine. Makes 2 large glasses.

Like a southern belle with a headache, this is a smooth lady with bite.

spiky peach

8 peaches, stones removed
1 small pineapple, peeled and chopped
10 g (1/2 cup) mint leaves
2 cm (3/4 inch) piece ginger

Juice the peaches, pineapple, mint and ginger through a juice extractor. Stir to combine. Makes 2 large glasses.

After one cocktail too many, the road to recovery is definitely orange.

carrot cocktail

10–12 carrots
125 ml ($1/2$ cup) pineapple juice
125 ml ($1/2$ cup) orange juice
1–2 teaspoons honey, to taste
8 ice cubes

Juice the carrots through a juice extractor.
Stir through the pineapple juice,
orange juice, honey and ice cubes.
Makes 2 medium glasses.

For a liquorice sting, choose a larger bulb of fennel.

orange and fennel juice

8 oranges
150 g (5^1/$_2$ oz) baby fennel

Peel and quarter the oranges, and remove any seeds. Juice the fennel through a juice extractor to release the flavours, then juice the orange and chill well. Stir to combine. Makes 2 medium glasses.

Note: When in season, the flavour will be stronger in larger, more developed fennel.

Too good for you? There's simply no such thing.

too good for you

6 carrots
1 large apple, cored
4 celery stalks, including leaves
6 iceberg lettuce leaves
20 English spinach leaves
ice cubes, to serve

Juice the carrots, apple, celery, lettuce and spinach through a juice extractor. Stir to combine and serve over ice. Makes 4 small glasses.

Beet yourself up at the end of winter and get yourself into the mood for spring.

spring clean

2 large cucumbers, peeled
6 carrots
1 large green apple, stalk removed
2 celery stalks, including leaves
1 large beetroot, scrubbed
ice cubes, to serve

Juice the cucumbers, carrots, apple, celery and beetroot through a juice extractor. Stir to combine and serve over ice. Makes 4 small glasses.

Add body and bounce to your natural vitality with this spicy beetroot booster.

beetroot, carrot and ginger juice

1 beetroot, scrubbed
6 carrots
3 cm (1¹/4 inch) piece ginger, peeled

Juice the beetroot, carrots and ginger through a juice extractor. Stir to combine. Makes 2 small glasses.

Cleanse your palate and freshen your breath with a powerful hit of parsley.

celery, parsley and tomato juice

20 g (1 cup) parsley
6 vine-ripened tomatoes
4 celery stalks
celery stalks, extra, to garnish

Juice the parsley, tomatoes and celery through a juice extractor. Chill well, then stir to combine. Serve garnished with a celery stalk swizzle stick. Makes 2 large glasses.

Note: For extra spice, add a few drops of Tabasco and freshly ground black pepper.

Sweet as honey and soft as dew, you know this drink's just right for you.

honeydew punch

1/2 honeydew melon, peeled, seeded and chopped
1 green apple, cored
2 oranges, peeled
ice cubes, to serve

Juice the honeydew, apple and oranges through a juice extractor. Stir to combine and serve over ice. Makes 2 small glasses.

Open your eyes to the joy of a long, cool, liquid breakfast.

watermelon breakfast juice

700 g (3½ cups) chopped watermelon
2 tablespoons lime juice
1–2 cm (½–¾ inch) piece ginger,
grated, to taste
2 tablespoons chopped mint

Blend the watermelon, lime juice, ginger and mint in a blender in short bursts — be careful not to overblend or the mixture will go frothy. Makes 2 large glasses.

Just what you need to get yourself into gear when time is short and the to-do list is long.

pineapple ginger kick

½ pineapple, peeled and chopped
3 oranges, peeled
3.5 cm (1½ inch) piece ginger
ice cubes, to serve

Juice the pineapple, oranges and ginger through a juice extractor. Stir to combine and serve over ice. Makes 2 small glasses.

Tarty, sweet grannies blend in perfect harmony with ruby rich raspberries.

raspberry and apple juice

150 g (5½ oz) raspberries
6 Granny Smith apples, stalks removed
ice cubes, to serve
mint sprigs, to garnish

Juice the raspberries and apples through a juice extractor. Pour into a jug and chill. Stir to combine and serve over ice, garnished with mint sprigs. Makes 2 medium glasses.

For a frisson of excitement, turn up the heat!

lime and chilli crush

6 limes, peeled
20 g (1 cup) mint leaves
2 teaspoons caster (superfine) sugar
ice cubes, to serve
1 chilli, halved lengthways and seeded

Juice the limes and mint through a juice extractor. Stir through the sugar and 125 ml ($^1/_2$ cup) chilled water until the sugar has dissolved. Fill 2 medium glasses with ice and place half a chilli in each. Pour in the juice and stir, pressing the chilli gently with a spoon to release some heat. Makes 2 medium glasses.

An apple a day keeps the doctor away … so double up and get ahead.

pear, apple and ginger juice

3 pears, cored
5 Granny Smith apples, stalks removed
3 cm (1¼ inch) piece ginger

Juice the pears, apples and ginger through a juice extractor. Stir to combine. Makes 2 medium glasses.

This is for those days when you just can't make up your mind.

sweet and sour

4 vine-ripened tomatoes
3 oranges, peeled
10 g (1/2 cup) mint leaves
1 teaspoon caster (superfine) sugar
1 teaspoon balsamic vinegar
ice cubes, to serve

Juice the tomatoes, oranges and mint through a juice extractor. Stir through the sugar and balsamic vinegar until the sugar has dissolved. Serve over ice. Makes 2 medium glasses.

Buff up for the beach with a nutrient-heavy detox draught.

summer detox

2 peaches
3 oranges, peeled
250 g (9 oz) strawberries, hulled
300 g (10½ oz) red seedless grapes

Cut a cross in the base of the peaches. Put them in a heatproof bowl and cover with boiling water. Leave for 1–2 minutes, then remove with a slotted spoon and plunge into cold water. Remove the skin and stones, and chop the flesh. Juice the oranges, strawberries, grapes and peaches through a juice extractor. Stir to combine and serve with long spoons. Makes 2 medium glasses.

If it's all been a bit of a blur so far, let this tangy blend set you straight.

morning blended fruit juice

1/2 pineapple, peeled and chopped
1 large pear, stalk removed
1 banana, chopped
40 g (1 1/2 oz) chopped pawpaw
375 ml (1 1/2 cups) orange juice

Blend the pineapple, pear, banana, pawpaw and orange juice in a blender until smooth. Makes 4 medium glasses.

Lacking passion with your honey? Just prepare, serve and look out.

honeydew melon and passionfruit

1 honeydew melon, peeled, seeded
and chopped
6 passionfruit, halved (see Note)
ice cubes, to serve

Juice the honeydew through a juice extractor. Scoop out the passionfruit pulp and stir through the juice. Chill well. Stir well to combine and serve in a jug with lots of ice. Makes 2 medium glasses.

Note: You will need 120 g (4¹/₂ oz) passionfruit pulp. If the passionfruit are not particularly juicy, you may need to add some canned passionfruit pulp.

This refreshing, slightly tart drink is perfect for a picnic — blend with ice, fill a thermos and quench your thirst all day!

lemon and green apple thirst quencher

80 ml (^{1}/$_2$ cup) lemon juice
6 green apples, stalks removed
mint leaves, to garnish

Pour the lemon juice into a serving jug. Juice the apples through a juice extractor. Add the apple juice to the lemon juice and stir to combine. Serve garnished with mint leaves. Makes 2 medium glasses.

Peppermint is well known as a stomach calmer and its fresh aroma can also lift your mood.

pear, melon and peppermint juice

3 pears, peeled and cored
1/2 small rockmelon (netted/US cantaloupe), peeled, seeded and chopped
few peppermint leaves
ice cubes, to serve

Juice the pears, rockmelon and peppermint through a juice extractor. Stir to combine and serve over ice. Makes 2 medium glasses.

Note: The best way to select a ripe melon is to use your nose — if it has a strong sweet fragrance and thick raised netting you can almost guarantee it is ready to eat.

Thick and smooth, this drink gently nudges mind and body into the new day.

peach and rockmelon juice

4 peaches
1/2 rockmelon (netted/US cantaloupe), peeled, seeded and chopped
600 ml (21 fl oz) orange juice
12 ice cubes
1 tablespoon lime juice

Cut a cross in the base of the peaches. Put them in a heatproof bowl and cover with boiling water. Leave for 1–2 minutes, then remove with a slotted spoon and plunge into cold water. Remove the skin and stones, and chop the flesh into bite-size pieces. Blend the peaches, rockmelon, orange juice and ice cubes in a blender until smooth. If the juice is too thick, add a little iced water. Stir through the lime juice. Makes 2 large glasses.

sparklies + fizzes

This sparkling little spritzer will put a spring in your step.

lemon, lime and soda with citrus ice cubes

1 lemon
1 lime
2¹/2 tablespoons lemon juice
170 ml (²/3 cup) lime juice cordial
625 ml (2¹/2 cups) soda water

Using a sharp knife, remove the zest and white pith from the lemon and lime. Cut between the membranes to release the segments. Put a lemon and lime segment in each hole of an ice-cube tray and cover with water. Freeze for 2–3 hours, or until firm. Combine the lemon juice, lime juice cordial and soda water. Pour into 2 glasses and add the ice cubes. Makes 2 medium glasses.

It's sweet, it's rich and it's full of what you need. What's not to fall for?

blueberry crush

150 g (5¹/₂ oz) blueberries
750 ml (3 cups) apple and blackcurrant juice
500 ml (2 cups) soda water
1 tablespoon caster (superfine) sugar
ice cubes, to serve

Blend the blueberries, apple and blackcurrant juice, soda water and sugar in a blender until smooth. Serve over ice. Makes 4 medium glasses.

Note: To make a slushy, add the ice cubes when blending the other ingredients.

A delightful mix of tart and fizzy, serve in tulip champagne glasses as a light dessert.

ruby grapefruit and lemon sorbet fizz

500 ml (2 cups) ruby grapefruit juice
250 ml (1 cup) soda water
1 tablespoon caster (superfine) sugar
4 scoops lemon sorbet

Combine the grapefruit juice, soda water and sugar in a jug and chill. Pour into 4 glasses and top each with a scoop of sorbet. Makes 4 small glasses.

Juice in bulk and fill your best bowl — your guests will be pleased as punch.

apricot fruit spritzer

500 ml (2 cups) apricot nectar
250 ml (1 cup) apple juice
250 ml (1 cup) orange juice
500 ml (2 cups) soda water
8 ice cubes

Put the apricot nectar, apple juice, orange juice, soda water and ice cubes into a large jug and stir to combine. Makes 4 medium glasses.

Just a sip of this fizzy fruity tongue tingler will transport anyone to a tropical island.

tropical kiwi sparkler

4 kiwifruit, peeled
500 ml (2 cups) tropical fruit juice
250 ml (1 cup) pineapple juice
ice cubes, to serve
sparkling mineral water, chilled, to serve
strawberries, chopped, to serve
kiwifruit, extra, to serve
small mint leaves, to garnish

Blend the kiwifruit in a blender until smooth. Add the tropical fruit juice and pineapple juice and blend until combined. Chill. Pour over ice into 6 large glasses and top with sparkling mineral water. Add the strawberries and kiwifruit, then garnish with the mint. Makes 6 large glasses.

Perhaps the next best thing to being hand fed grapes ...

grape refresher

60 ml (¹/4 cup) caster (superfine) sugar
1 litre (4 cups) dark grape juice
60 ml (¹/4 cup) lemon juice
ice cubes, to serve
sparkling mineral water, to serve
lemon slices, to garnish
12 seedless green grapes, to garnish, optional

Place the sugar and grape juice in a large saucepan and stir over medium heat until the sugar has dissolved. Stir through the lemon juice and refrigerate until cold. Pour over ice into 6 tall glasses to three-quarters full and top with sparkling mineral water and a lemon slice. Cut the grapes in half, thread among 6 wooden skewers and place over each glass, if desired. Makes 6 tall glasses.

If you adore mangoes but can't abide the juice dribbling down your arms, call in the blender.

mango summer haze

2 mangoes, peeled, stones removed
and chopped
500 ml (2 cups) orange juice
55 g (¼ cup) caster (superfine) sugar
500 ml (2 cups) sparkling mineral water
ice cubes, to serve
mango slices, to garnish, optional

Blend the mango, orange juice and sugar in a blender until smooth. Stir through the mineral water. Serve over ice and garnish with fresh mango slices, if desired. Makes 6 large glasses.

Pale pink and lime green isn't always a fashion winner but here it's definitely à la mode.

guava juice and soda with zested lime blocks

zest and juice of 2 limes
2 tablespoons lime cordial
500 ml (2 cups) soda water
750 ml (3 cups) guava juice

Put the lime juice, lime cordial and half the soda water into a jug and mix together. Pour into an ice-cube tray and top each cube with a little of the lime zest. Freeze until solid. Divide the ice cubes among 4 glasses and top with the combined guava juice and remaining soda water. Makes 4 medium glasses.

Note: The colour of guava flesh will vary from pale yellow to soft pink. We used pink for this drink as it tends to be sweeter and have a slightly stronger fragrance.

Bewitch yourself with this tingly little teaser.

fresh pineapple juice with mandarin sorbet

1 large pineapple, peeled and chopped
250 ml (1 cup) dry ginger ale
4 scoops mandarin sorbet

Juice the pineapple through a juice extractor. Combine the pineapple juice and dry ginger ale in a large jug and chill. Stir to combine, pour into 2 glasses and top each with 2 scoops of sorbet. Makes 2 medium glasses.

Mangoes have never had it so good — cosseted by fizzy sweetness.

mango and mandarin chill

1 mango, peeled, stone removed and sliced
500 ml (2 cups) mandarin juice
125 ml (1/2 cup) lime juice cordial
375 ml (1 1/2 cups) soda water
2 tablespoons caster (superfine) sugar
ice cubes, to serve

Freeze the mango for about 1 hour, or until semi-frozen. Combine the mandarin juice, cordial, soda water and sugar in a jug. Put the mango slices and some ice cubes into 2 glasses, then pour in the juice mixture. Makes 2 medium glasses.

Note: For those with a sensitive sweet tooth, add the sugar to taste at the end.

For a nightlife moment without the morning after, kick back with a sober mule.

sober mule

3 grapefruit, peeled
7 g (1/3 cup) mint leaves
375 ml (11/2 cups) ginger beer
ice cubes, to serve
2 small mint sprigs, to garnish

Juice the grapefruit and mint through a juice extractor. Stir through the ginger beer and serve over ice, garnished with mint. Makes 2 large glasses.

Revisit your cider-fuelled student years without the grungy flat mates.

apple fizz

6 apples, stalks removed
1 lemon, peeled
250 ml (1 cup) apple cider
ice cubes, to serve

Juice the apples and lemon through a juice extractor. Stir through the apple cider and serve over ice. Makes 2 large glasses.

They say it takes two to tango,
so try not to drink this
on your own.

mango tango

2 mangoes, peeled, stones removed
1 small pineapple, peeled and chopped
2 panama or large passionfruit, halved
375 ml (1^1/$_2$ cups) sparkling grape juice

Juice the mangoes and pineapple through a juice extractor. Scoop out the passionfruit pulp and stir through the grape juice. Makes 2 large glasses.

Yummy plummy in your tummy keeps you on the go.

plum and basil tango

10 small plums, stones removed
2 limes, peeled
10 g ($^1/_3$ cup) basil leaves
375 ml (1$^1/_2$ cups) lemonade
ice cubes, to serve
basil leaves, extra, to garnish

Juice the plums, limes and basil through a juice extractor. Stir through the lemonade. Serve over ice, garnished with basil leaves. Makes 2 large glasses.

Get to know this kiwi sparkler and it could be the beginning of a beautiful friendship.

lime and kiwi sparkler

2 limes, peeled
9 kiwifruit, peeled
375 ml (1½ cups) dry ginger ale
ice cubes, to serve
mint sprigs, to garnish
lime slices, to garnish

Juice the limes and kiwifruit through a juice extractor. Stir through the dry ginger ale and serve over ice with a mint sprig and lime slices. Makes 2 large glasses.

Add heat to sun-warmed peaches with a pinch of spicy nutmeg.

fuzzy peach

6 peaches, stones removed
1 lemon, peeled
large pinch freshly grated nutmeg
250 ml (1 cup) dry ginger ale
ice cubes, to serve

Juice the peaches and lemon through a juice extractor. Stir through the nutmeg and dry ginger ale. Serve over ice. Makes 2 large glasses.

Clean, crisp lychees hook up with earthy passionfruit for an affair worth remembering.

lychee passion fizz

500 g (1 lb 2 oz) lychees, peeled and seeded
2 cm (3/4 inch) piece ginger
3 large passionfruit, halved
500 ml (2 cups) lemonade or soda water

Juice the lychees and ginger through a juice extractor. Scoop out the passionfruit pulp and stir through the lemonade or soda water. Makes 2 large glasses.

The ultimate classic combo, give peaches and cream a modern makeover.

peach nectar spider fluff

600 ml (21 fl oz) peach nectar
600 ml (21 fl oz) soda water
4 scoops vanilla ice cream
1 peach, sliced

Combine the peach nectar and soda water in a jug. Pour into 4 tall glasses, top each with a scoop of ice cream and garnish with peach slices. Makes 4 medium glasses.

Suck it in and prepare for the sour cherry punch.

sweet-tart

250 ml (1 cup) blood orange juice
125 ml (1/2 cup) sour cherry juice
1 tablespoon lime juice
250 ml (1 cup) soda water
ice cubes, to serve

Combine the blood orange juice, sour cherry juice and lime juice in a jug. Stir through the soda water and serve over ice. Makes 2 large glasses.

Serve this delicate, dainty drink after a long afternoon on the croquet lawn.

mandarin rose

375 ml (1¹/2 cups) mandarin juice
1 teaspoon rosewater
2 teaspoons pomegranate syrup
250 ml (1 cup) soda water or lemonade
ice cubes, to serve

Combine the mandarin juice, rosewater, pomegranate syrup and soda water or lemonade in a jug. Serve over ice. Makes 2 large glasses.

Sweet yet slightly astringent, this drink can catch you off guard.

pineapple delight

1/2 pineapple, peeled and chopped
2 cups (500 ml) lemonade
2 tablespoons lime juice
mint leaves, to garnish

Blend the pineapple in a blender for 1–2 minutes, or until as smooth as possible. Pour the lemonade into a jug and gently stir through the pineapple purée. Add the lime juice and mix well. Serve garnished with the mint. Makes 4 small glasses.

Sweet red fruit sings with the deep bass notes of cold black tea.

cherry and berry punch

400 g (2 cups) cherries, pitted
200 g (7 oz) blackberries
200 g (7 oz) blueberries
125 g (4$^1/2$ oz) strawberries, hulled
and halved
750 ml (3 cups) dry ginger ale
500 ml (2 cups) lemonade
250 ml (1 cup) cold black tea
zest of 1 lemon, cut into long thin strips
10 mint leaves, torn
ice cubes, to serve

Put the cherries, blackberries, blueberries, strawberries, dry ginger ale, lemonade, tea, lemon zest and mint into a jug. Cover the jug and chill for at least 3 hours. Add ice cubes to serve. Makes 10 small glasses.

frappés + freezies

Mouth-puckeringly tart when consumed straight, a shot of sugar makes tamarind lip-smackingly good.

tamarind cooler

2 teaspoons tamarind concentrate
3 tablespoons caster (superfine) sugar
20 g (1 cup) mint leaves
12 large ice cubes

Blend the tamarind, sugar, mint, ice cubes and 250 ml (1 cup) water in a blender until smooth. Makes 2 medium glasses.

All work and no play is never a good idea — this drink helps factor in a little r'n'r.

r'n'r

300 g (10½ oz) frozen raspberries
juice of 1 lime
½ rockmelon (netted/US cantaloupe),
peeled, seeded and chopped
1 teaspoon honey

Blend the frozen raspberries with the lime juice in a blender in short bursts until starting to break up. Add the rockmelon and honey and blend until smooth. Makes 2 medium glasses.

It's creamy, it's cold and it's berry good.

berry cheesecake slushy

300 g (10^1/$_2$ oz) frozen blueberries
150 g (5^1/$_2$ oz) raspberries
200 g (7 oz) vanilla yoghurt
250 ml (1 cup) milk
1 tablespoon wheat germ

Blend the frozen blueberries in a blender in short bursts until starting to break up. Add the raspberries, yoghurt, milk and wheat germ and blend until smooth. Makes 2 large glasses.

Choose a sweet, mellow golden apple variety that will let the raspberries shine.

raspapple freezie

6 apples, stalks removed or 500 ml (2 cups) apple juice
300 g (10 1/2 oz) frozen raspberries

Juice the apples through a juice extractor. Blend the apple juice and frozen raspberries in a blender until smooth. Makes 2 large glasses.

Smooth, thick and calming, consider using any leftovers as a facial!

papaya, date and almond crush

1/2 papaya, peeled, seeds removed and chopped
4 fresh dates, pitted
375 ml (1 1/2 cups) almond milk
1 teaspoon rosewater
8 large ice cubes

Blend the papaya, dates, almond milk, rosewater and ice cubes in a blender until smooth. Makes 2 medium glasses.

Papa don't preach, I'm taking good care of myself with a healthy dose of papaya.

papaya and coconut frappé

½ papaya, peeled, seeded and chopped
400 ml (14 fl oz) coconut milk
2 tablespoons lime juice
2 tablespoons caster (superfine) sugar
1 teaspoon natural vanilla extract (essence)
pinch allspice
8 large ice cubes

Blend the payaya, coconut milk, lime juice, sugar, vanilla, allspice and ice cubes in a blender until smooth. Makes 2 large glasses.

A floating cloud of fruity heaven, perfect for drifting along on a sunny afternoon.

strawberry, kiwi and peach slushy

250 g (9 oz) strawberries, hulled
2 kiwifruit, peeled and chopped
200 g (7 oz) canned peaches in natural juice
3 scoops orange sorbet or gelato

Blend the strawberries, kiwifruit, undrained peaches and sorbet or gelato in a blender until smooth. Makes 2 large glasses.

Discover the delights of the frozen fruit section and conjure up summer with this creamy concoction.

cranberry, raspberry and vanilla slushy

500 ml (2 cups) cranberry juice
300 g (10^1/$_2$ oz) frozen raspberries
1 tablespoon caster (superfine) sugar
200 g (7 oz) vanilla yoghurt

Blend the cranberry juice, frozen raspberries, sugar and yoghurt in a blender until smooth. Makes 2 large glasses.

Note: To make your own vanilla yoghurt, simply scrape the seeds from a vanilla bean into a large tub of natural yoghurt, add the pod and refrigerate overnight. Remove the pod before serving.

Give 'em the old razzle dazzle
and watch 'em come
back for more.

razzle dazzle

1 lime
150 g (5¹/₂ oz) raspberries
1 teaspoon natural vanilla extract (essence)
200 g (7 oz) strawberry frozen yoghurt

Juice the lime in a citrus press. Blend the raspberries, lime juice, vanilla and frozen yoghurt in a blender until smooth. Makes 2 small glasses.

Factor in 8 scoops of sorbet — one for the blender, one for me, one for the blender …

banana, kiwi and lemon frappé

2 bananas, chopped
3 kiwifruit, peeled and chopped
4 scoops lemon sorbet

Blend the banana, kiwifruit and lemon sorbet in a blender until smooth. Makes 2 medium glasses.

Use the best maple syrup you can find, then make this for your favourite mountie.

pear, maple and cinnamon frappé

400 g (14 oz) canned pears in natural juice
1 1/2 tablespoons pure maple syrup
1/2 teaspoon ground cinnamon
12 large ice cubes

Blend the undrained pears, maple syrup, cinnamon and ice cubes in a blender until smooth. Makes 2 large glasses.

I've got a lovely bunch of coconuts so let's make some ice, ice, baby.

coconut and lime ice

400 ml (14 fl oz) coconut milk
juice of 4 limes
2 teaspoons natural vanilla extract (essence)
80 g ($1/3$ cup) caster (superfine) sugar
7 g ($1/3$ cup) mint leaves, optional
8 large ice cubes

Blend the coconut milk, lime juice, vanilla, sugar, mint and ice cubes in a blender until smooth. Makes 2 large glasses.

A veritable bazaar of flavours — sweet, nutty and smooth as a bolt of silk.

whipped nougat

200 g (1 cup) canned apricots
500 ml (2 cups) almond milk
1$1/2$ teaspoons natural vanilla extract (essence)
1 teaspoons of honey
few drops rosewater, optional
8 large ice cubes

Blend the undrained apricots, almond milk, vanilla, honey, rosewater and ice cubes in a blender until smooth. Makes 2 large glasses.

Serve with sushi on a Friday night and say sayonara baby to the working week.

cherry blossom slushy

3 large Nashi pears, stalks removed
300 g (10½ oz) frozen pitted cherries

Juice the Nashi pears through a juice extractor. Blend the Nashi juice and frozen cherries in a blender until smooth. Makes 2 medium glasses.

Almond milk is saved for special occasions in the Middle East but don't let that stop you from making this as often as you want.

grape and almond frappé

500 g (1 lb 2 oz) green seedless grapes
250 ml (1 cup) almond milk
large pinch ground cinnamon
8 large ice cubes

Juice the grapes through a juice extractor. Blend the grape juice, almond milk, cinnamon and ice cubes in a blender until smooth. Makes 2 medium glasses.

Note: Almonds are high in calcium and an excellent inclusion in a dairy-free diet.

The wrinklier the passionfruit, the sweeter the pulp, so get down with an oldie.

passionfruit lime crush

125 ml (1/2 cup) passionfruit pulp (about 6 passionfruit)
185 ml (3/4 cup) lime juice cordial
750 ml (3 cups) dry ginger ale
crushed ice, to serve

Combine the passionfruit pulp, cordial and dry ginger ale in a large jug and mix together well. Half fill 4 large glasses with crushed ice and add the passionfruit mixture. Makes 4 large glasses.

This drink is a terribly good tipple in its own right, but if you must add a slug of vodka, we promise not to tell.

virgin mary

750 ml (3 cups) tomato juice
1 tablespoon Worcestershire sauce
2 tablespoons lemon juice
1/4 teaspoon ground nutmeg
few drops of Tabasco
12 ice cubes
2 lemon slices, halved

Put the tomato juice, Worcestershire sauce, lemon juice, nutmeg and Tabasco sauce in a large jug and stir to combine. Blend the ice cubes in a blender for 30 seconds, or until the ice is crushed to 125 ml (1/2 cup). Pour the tomato juice mixture into 4 glasses and add the crushed ice and lemon slices. Season with salt and pepper. Makes 4 small glasses.

Aloha summer, here we come.

hawaiian crush

100 g (3¹/₂ oz) papaya, peeled, seeded and chopped
200 g (1 cup) chopped watermelon
250 ml (1 cup) apple juice
6 large ice cubes

Blend the papaya, watermelon, apple juice and ice cubes in a blender until smooth. Chill well. Makes 2 medium glasses.

Think you're too old for an ice cream spider? Try this grown-up version.

orange and lemon sorbet soda

500 ml (2 cups) orange juice
250 ml (1 cup) lemonade
2–4 scoops lemon sorbet

Combine the orange juice and lemonade in a jug. Pour into 2 large glasses and top each with 1–2 scoops sorbet. Makes 2 large glasses

Mint plucked fresh from the plant is one of life's surest pick-me-ups.

pear and mint frappé

4 pears, peeled, cored and chopped
2 teaspoons roughly chopped mint leaves
3 teaspoons caster (superfine) sugar
30 ice cubes
mint leaves, to garnish

Blend the pears, mint and sugar in a blender until smooth. Add the ice cubes and blend until smooth. Serve garnished with the extra mint leaves. Makes 2 medium glasses.

Why mess with a classic?

coconut and lime lassi

400 ml (14 fl oz) coconut milk
185 g (3/4 cup) natural yoghurt
60 ml (1/4 cup) lime juice
55 g (1/4 cup) caster (superfine) sugar
8–10 ice cubes
lime slices, to garnish

Blend the coconut milk, yoghurt, lime juice, sugar and ice cubes in a blender until well combined and smooth. Serve garnished with lime slices. Makes 2 medium glasses.

Note: Use strong, creamy yoghurt to make sure the lassi has tang.

Enjoy a thousand-and-one Arabian nights with this petal-scented sparkler.

watermelon rosewater slushy

600 g (3 cups) chopped watermelon
1 teaspoon rosewater
1 teaspoon lemon juice
500 ml (2 cups) lemonade

Blend the watermelon in a blender until smooth. Combine with the rosewater, lemon juice and lemonade, then pour into a shallow metal tray. Cover with plastic wrap and freeze for 2 hours, or until just solid around the edges. Return to the blender and blend until thick and slushy. Makes 4 large glasses.

Note: Watermelons are now available almost all year, but tend to be sweeter in the warmer months. Choose one that feels heavy for its size.

Sprinkled with a few orange nasturtium petals, this drink is almost too pretty to drink. Almost.

papaya crush with lime sorbet

300 g (10½ oz) chopped red papaya
1–2 tablespoons lime juice
4 scoops lime sorbet
crushed ice
lime zest, to garnish

Blend the papaya, lime juice, 2 scoops of lime sorbet and some crushed ice in a blender until thick and smooth. Pour into 2 tall glasses and top each with a scoop of sorbet. Garnish with lime zest and serve with spoons. Makes 2 large glasses.

Note: There is much confusion about the difference between papaya and pawpaw. We used here a red papaya — a small, pear-shaped fruit with red-orange flesh.

If you're feeling truly indulgent, serve this luscious frappé over ice cream for a tropical fantasy.

tropical fruit frappé

160 g (1 cup) chopped pineapple
¼ small rockmelon (netted/US cantaloupe), peeled, seeded and chopped
1 banana, chopped
180 g (1 cup) chopped pawpaw
1 mango, peeled, stone removed and chopped
250 ml (1 cup) pineapple juice
crushed ice

Blend the pineapple, rockmelon, banana, pawpaw and mango in a blender until smooth. Add the pineapple juice and crushed ice and blend until the frappé is thick and the ice has thoroughly broken down. Makes 4 medium glasses.

Note: This makes a great breakfast in a glass. The fruit must be ripe or you'll need to add sugar. Add a little coconut milk if you prefer a creamy drink.

If only all of our crushes could be so sweet.

orange citrus crush

12 navel oranges
zest and juice of 1 lime
sugar, to taste
ice cubes, to serve

Segment 2 of the oranges and juice the remainder in a citrus press — don't strain the juice, you can keep the pulp in it. Add the lime zest and lime juice to the orange juice. Add the orange segments and sugar, stir to combine and serve over ice.
Makes 4 medium glasses.

Note: The juice of navel (seedless) oranges will turn bitter within minutes of juicing, so drink it immediately. Use blood oranges when they're in season.

All the colours of the rainbow swirled together in a happy frappé.

orange and mixed fruit frappé

10 dried apricot halves
200 g (7 oz) raspberries
1 banana, chopped
1 mango, chopped
500 ml (2 cups) orange juice
1 tablespoon mint leaves
6 ice cubes

Put the dried apricots in a heatproof bowl with 60 ml ($1/4$ cup) boiling water. Set aside for 10 minutes, or until plump, then drain and roughly chop. Blend the apricots, raspberries, banana, mango, orange juice, mint and ice cubes in a blender until thick and smooth. Makes 4 medium glasses.

Get your motor running with this energy blast.

banana starter

2 bananas, chopped
100 g (3$\frac{1}{2}$ oz) frozen blueberries
1 red apple, cored and chopped
300 ml (10$\frac{1}{2}$ fl oz) apple juice
2 ice cubes

Blend the banana, blueberries, apple, apple juice and ice cubes in a blender until smooth. Makes 4 small glasses.

Choose plump kiwifruit with a little give in them.

kiwi delight

3 kiwifruit, peeled and sliced
80 g (1/2 cup) chopped pineapple
1 banana, chopped
250 ml (1 cup) tropical fruit juice
2 ice cubes

Blend the kiwifruit, pineapple, banana, fruit juice and ice cubes in a blender until smooth. Makes 4 small glasses.

Cool down on a sultry afternoon with a long, deep sip of this frosty freshener.

melon freezie

1/3 honeydew melon, peeled, seeded and chopped
1/2 small rockmelon (netted/US cantaloupe), peeled, seeded and chopped
12 ice cubes
500 ml (2 cups) orange juice

Blend the honeydew and rockmelon in a blender for 1 minute, or until smooth. Add the ice cubes and orange juice and blend for a further 30 seconds. Transfer to a large shallow plastic dish and freeze for 3 hours. Return to the blender and blend quickly until smooth. Serve with straws and long spoons. Makes 4 medium glasses.

Note: Roughly break up the ice cubes first by placing them in a clean tea towel and hitting on a hard surface.

Think plump and juicy when choosing strawberries. Repeat out loud: plump and juicy.

watermelon and strawberry slushy

2 kg (10 cups) chopped watermelon
(1 large watermelon)
250 g (9 oz) strawberries, hulled
2 teaspoons caster (superfine) sugar

Combine the watermelon, strawberries and sugar in a bowl. Blend the mixture in batches in a blender until smooth, then pour into a shallow metal tray. Cover with plastic wrap and freeze for 2–3 hours, or until the mixture begins to freeze. Return to the blender and blend quickly to break up the ice. Makes 6 medium glasses.

shakes + smoothies

Okay, so this is not for the dieters, but that's just the way it is in life.

cherrycoco

400 g (2 cups) cherries, pitted
400 ml (14 fl oz) coconut milk
2 teaspoons caster (superfine) sugar
1 teaspoon natural vanilla extract (essence)
ice cubes, to serve

Juice the cherries though a juice extractor. Mix well with the coconut milk, sugar and vanilla. Serve over ice. Makes 2 small glasses.

Note: You could use vanilla sugar in this recipe — just keep a vanilla bean in a jar of sugar for fragrant sugar.

Add a plate of shortbread and some whipped cream for a pared-down take on the real thing.

vanilla apple pie

3 apples, stalks removed or 250 ml (1 cup) apple juice
200 g (7 oz) canned pie apple
2 scoops vanilla ice cream
1/2 teaspoon ground cinnamon
1 teaspoon natural vanilla extract (essence)
ground cinnamon or freshly grated nutmeg, to serve, optional

Juice the apples through a juice extractor. Blend the juice, pie apple, ice cream, cinnamon and vanilla in a blender until smooth. Serve sprinkled with cinnamon or nutmeg, if desired. Makes 2 medium glasses.

If things have been a little on the upset side, revive an overworked stomach with potassium-rich banana.

banana, kiwi and mint smoothie

2 bananas, chopped
2 kiwifruit, peeled and chopped
5 g (1/4 cup) mint leaves
250 ml (1 cup) milk or coconut milk
2 scoops vanilla ice cream

Blend the banana, kiwifruit, mint, milk and ice cream in a blender until smooth. Makes 2 medium glasses.

Delight your inner child, or even a real one, with this modern take on one of the classic old favourites.

apricot crumble smoothie

200 g (7 oz) canned apricots
200 g (7 oz) vanilla yoghurt
250 ml (1 cup) milk
1 tablespoon wheat germ
1 tablespoon malted milk powder
large pinch ground cinnamon

Blend the undrained apricots, yoghurt, milk, wheat germ, malted milk powder and cinnamon in a blender until smooth. Makes 2 large glasses.

Note: Canned peaches, apples or pears can be used in place of the apricots.

The power of caramel and malt to make some of us go week at the knees should never be underestimated.

caramelized banana shake

2 bananas, chopped
500 ml (2 cups) milk
2 scoops ice cream
1¹/₂ tablespoons caramel sauce
1 tablespoon malted milk powder
pinch ground cinnamon

Blend the banana, milk, ice cream, caramel sauce, malted milk powder and cinnamon in a blender until smooth. Makes 2 large glasses.

Meal replacement therapy never tasted so good.

mixed berry protein punch

250 g (9 oz) mixed berries (strawberries, raspberries, blueberries)
1 tablespoon protein powder
200 g (7 oz) vanilla yoghurt
375 ml (1 1/2 cups) milk
2 tablespoons ground almonds

Blend the berries, protein powder, yoghurt, milk and ground almonds in a blender until smooth. Makes 2 large glasses.

Use a light floral honey so you don't overwhelm the delicate flavour of the custard apple.

custard apple smoothie

2 custard apples, peeled and seeded
500 ml (2 cups) milk
2 teaspoons honey
1 1/2 teaspoons natural vanilla extract (essence)
1 teaspoon rosewater
ice cubes, to serve

Blend the custard apples, milk, honey, vanilla and rosewater in a blender until smooth. Serve over ice. Makes 2 large glasses.

The avocado, master of disguise, is a fruit that packs a protein punch.

avocado smoothie

1 small avocado, peeled, stone removed
500 ml (2 cups) milk
3 teaspoons honey
1/2 teaspoon natural vanilla extract (essence)

Blend the avocado, milk, honey and vanilla in a blender until smooth. Makes 2 medium glasses.

One of these once a week will keep you as regular as clockwork.

regulator

125 g (4½ oz) pitted prunes
honey, to taste, optional
ice cubes, to serve

Blend the prunes with 500 ml (2 cups) cold water in a blender until smooth. Stir through the honey, if desired. Strain and serve over ice. Makes 2 small glasses.

Calm a troubled tummy with this soothing tonic.

savoury soother

1 kg (2 lb 4 oz) cucumbers
1 lime, peeled
10 g ($1/3$ cup) coriander (cilantro) leaves
1 garlic clove
1 small avocado, peeled, stone removed
large pinch ground cumin

Juice the cucumbers, lime, coriander and garlic through a juice extractor. Transfer to a blender with the avocado and cumin and blend until smooth. Makes 2 small glasses.

Figs are the fruit of love so serve this up for that someone special.

fig and ginger dream

6 small fresh figs
30 g (1 oz) ginger in syrup, plus
1 teaspoon syrup
625 ml (2 1/2 cups) milk
2 teaspoons natural vanilla extract (essence)
ice cubes, to serve

Blend the figs, ginger, syrup, milk and vanilla in a blender until smooth. Serve over ice. Makes 2 large glasses.

Sweet, smooth and a little bit nutty — sounds like an average day in the office.

banana sesame bender

3 small bananas, chopped
750 ml (3 cups) milk
1 1/2 tablespoons tahini
1 1/2 tablespoons peanut butter
1 tablespoon honey
2 teaspoons natural vanilla extract (essence)

Blend the banana, milk, tahini, peanut butter, honey and vanilla in a blender until smooth. Makes 2 large glasses.

Cherries seem so indulgent — this drink will do nothing to change that impression.

almond cherry smoothie

375 ml (1½ cups) almond milk
400 g (2 cups) cherries, pitted
¼ teaspoon natural vanilla extract (essence)
pinch ground cinnamon
4 large ice cubes

Blend the almond milk, cherries, vanilla, cinnamon and ice cubes in a blender until smooth. Makes 2 large glasses.

Note: If you like a strong almond or marzipan flavour, add a dash of almond extract (essence) to the blender.

Serve in a parfait glass with long spoons and curly straws for the true diner experience.

passionfruit and vanilla ice cream whip

4 passionfruit, halved
100 g (3^1/$_2$ oz) passionfruit yoghurt
500 ml (2 cups) milk
1 tablespoon caster (superfine) sugar
2–4 scoops vanilla ice cream

Scoop out the passionfruit pulp and push through a sieve to remove the seeds. Transfer to a blender with the yoghurt, milk, sugar and 2 scoops of ice cream and blend until smooth. Pour into 2 glasses and top each with an extra scoop of ice cream, if desired. Makes 2 medium glasses.

Do the hippy hippy shake with a luscious mound of melon.

melon shake

1/2 small rockmelon (netted/US cantaloupe),
peeled, seeded and chopped
5 scoops vanilla ice cream
375 ml (1 1/2 cups) milk
2 tablespoons honey
ground nutmeg, to serve

Blend the rockmelon in a blender for 30 seconds, or until smooth. Add the ice cream, milk and honey and blend for a further 10–20 seconds, or until well combined and smooth. Serve sprinkled with nutmeg. Makes 2 medium glasses.

Establish a new tradition at Christmas with this peachy take on an old classic.

peachy egg nog

2 eggs, separated
60 ml (1/4 cup) milk
55 g (1/4 cup) caster (superfine) sugar
80 ml (1/3 cup) cream
440 ml (13/4 cups) peach nectar
2 tablespoons orange juice
ground nutmeg, to garnish

Beat the yolks, milk and half the sugar in a bowl. Put over a pan of simmering water — do not allow the base to touch the water. Cook, stirring, for 8 minutes, or until the custard thickens. Remove from the heat and cover the surface with plastic wrap. Cool. Beat the egg whites until frothy. Add the remaining sugar, to taste, then beat into stiff peaks. In a separate bowl, whip the cream to soft peaks. Fold the cream and whites into the custard. Stir through the nectar and juice. Cover and chill for 2 hours. Beat lightly, then serve sprinkled with nutmeg. Makes 4 small glasses.

Coffee and breakfast in one easy package to start the morning with a blast.

banana soy latte

440 ml (1¾ cups) coffee-flavoured soy milk
2 bananas, chopped
8 large ice cubes
1 teaspoon drinking chocolate
¼ teaspoon ground cinnamon

Blend the soy milk and banana in a blender until smooth. With the blender running, add the ice cubes one at a time until well incorporated. Serve sprinkled with the drinking chocolate and cinnamon. Makes 4 small glasses.

Tangy buttermilk adds protein and oomph to this low-fat smoothie.

plum and prune tang

200 g (1/2 cup) chopped plums
150 g (1 cup) prunes, pitted and chopped
250 g (1 cup) low-fat vanilla yoghurt
125 ml (1/2 cup) buttermilk
310 ml (11/4 cups) skim milk
8 large ice cubes

Blend the plums, prunes, yoghurt, buttermilk, milk and ice cubes in a blender until smooth. Makes 4 small glasses.

When the island breeze is calling but work has you stalling, take an instant holiday with this tropical shake.

mango and coconut shake

400 g (14 oz) fresh mango flesh
125 ml (1/2 cup) lime juice
125 ml (1/2 cup) coconut milk
2 teaspoons honey
3 teaspoons finely chopped mint
12 large ice cubes

Blend the mango, lime juice, coconut milk, honey, mint and ice cubes in a blender until smooth. Chill well. Stir to combine. Makes 2 medium glasses.

For a kitsch centrepiece, serve this crazy coconut concoction in a hollowed-out pineapple.

coconut and pineapple iced drink

1 pineapple, peeled and chopped
250 ml (1 cup) coconut milk
mint leaves, to garnish
pineapple leaves, to garnish

Juice the pineapple through a juice extractor. Transfer to a large jug and stir through the coconut milk. Pour 125 ml (1/2 cup) of the mixture into 8 holes of an ice-cube tray and freeze. Chill the remaining mixture. When the ice cubes have frozen, pour the juice mixture into 2 glasses, add the ice cubes and garnish with mint and pineapple leaves. Makes 2 medium glasses.

If the muddy field is not your game, chill out on the sidelines with a thermos full of this.

sports shake

500 ml (2 cups) milk, chilled
2 tablespoons honey
2 eggs
$1/2$ teaspoon vanilla essence
1 tablespoon wheat germ
1 medium banana, sliced

Blend the milk, honey, eggs, vanilla, wheat germ and banana until smooth. Chill well and serve. Makes 2 large glasses.

Start the day in a relaxed way with this vitamin B-rich shake.

passionfruit breakfast shake

150 g (5¹/2 oz) passionfruit and other mixed
fruit (mango, banana, peaches,
strawberries, blueberries)
60 g (¹/4 cup) vanilla yoghurt
250 ml (1 cup) milk
2 teaspoons wheat germ
1 tablespoon honey
1 egg, optional
1 tablespoon malted milk powder

Blend the fruit, yoghurt, milk, wheat germ, honey, egg and malted milk powder in a blender for 30–60 seconds, or until well combined. Makes 2 medium glasses.

Whip these up for a kiddy occasion and you'll be the fairy godmother.

apple and blackcurrant shake

250 ml (1 cup) apple and blackcurrant juice
2 tablespoons natural yoghurt
185 ml (3/4 cup) milk
3 scoops vanilla ice cream

Blend the juice, yoghurt, milk and ice cream in a blender until well combined and fluffy. Makes 2 medium glasses.

Good ready-made custard is readily available so feel free to take the easy road to sweetie heaven.

cinnamon and custard shake

375 ml (1 1/2 cups) milk
185 ml (3/4 cup) ready-made custard
3 scoops vanilla ice cream
3 teaspoons honey
1 1/2 teaspoons ground cinnamon
ground cinnamon, extra, to serve

Blend the milk, custard, ice cream, honey and cinnamon until smooth and fluffy. Serve sprinkled with extra cinnamon. Makes 2 medium glasses.

If you've been good, reward yourself by using coconut cream for an extra luscious tipple.

island blend

110 g ($^2/_3$ cup) chopped pineapple
$^1/_2$ small papaya, peeled, seeded and chopped
2 small bananas, chopped
60 ml ($^1/_4$ cup) coconut milk
250 ml (1 cup) orange juice
ice cubes, to serve

Blend the pineapple, papaya, banana and coconut milk in a blender until smooth. Add the orange juice and blend until combined. Serve over ice. Makes 2 medium glasses.

Save a glass for your bath and soak your way to silky skin.

apricot and bran breakfast

100 g (3½ oz) dried apricots
1 tablespoon oat bran
60 g (¼ cup) apricot yoghurt
600 ml (21 fl oz) milk
1 tablespoon honey

Soak the dried apricots in boiling water until they are plump and rehydrated, then drain. Blend the apricots, bran, yoghurt, milk and honey in a blender until thick and smooth. Makes 2 large glasses.

A hot drink at bedtime is one of the few pleasures that lasts a lifetime.

creamy vanilla and almond shake

1 vanilla bean, halved lengthways
500 ml (2 cups) milk
80 g (1/2 cup) raw almonds, toasted
1 tablespoon pure maple syrup
1 teaspoon almond extract (essence)

Put the vanilla bean and milk in a saucepan and heat until almost boiling. Remove from the heat to infuse for 5 minutes, then return to the heat until almost boiling. Remove the bean. Blend the milk, almonds, maple syrup and almond extract in a blender until smooth, thick and creamy. Makes 2 medium glasses.

Note: Rinse the vanilla bean, let it dry and put it in an airtight container of caster (superfine) sugar. You could use this vanilla sugar in place of the maple syrup.

Like an iced vo-vo in a glass, this one takes us back to trampoline days. Bouncing is optional.

raspberry and coconut cream shake

200 g (7 oz) raspberries
250 ml (1 cup) apple and blackcurrant juice
400 ml (14 fl oz) coconut cream
2 scoops vanilla soy ice cream
marshmallows, to serve

Blend the raspberries, apple and blackcurrant juice, coconut cream and ice cream in a blender for several minutes until thick and creamy. Thread marshmallows onto 4 swizzle sticks and serve with the shakes, along with a straw and a long spoon. Makes 4 small glasses.

Note: For a low-fat drink, blend the raspberries and juice with ice instead of coconut cream and ice cream.

Just when winter thinks it's got you cornered, strike back with vitamin-rich, dried fruit.

pear and peach protein drink

3 dried pear halves
3 dried peach halves
1 egg
2 tablespoons low-fat peach yoghurt
400 ml (14 fl oz) skim milk
1 tablespoon malted milk powder
1 tablespoon ground almonds
ground cinnamon, to serve

Put the pears, peaches and 125 ml ($1/2$ cup) boiling water into a heatproof bowl. Set aside for 10 minutes, or until the fruit is plump and juicy. Drain the fruit, reserving the soaking liquid, and allow to cool. Chop the fruit and blend with the soaking liquid, egg, yoghurt, milk, malted milk powder and ground almonds in a blender until thick and smooth. Serve sprinkled with a little cinnamon. Makes 2 medium glasses.

No corny jokes about soy good for you — one mouthful and you know it's true.

fresh date and pear soy shake

400 ml (14 fl oz) creamy soy milk
4 fresh dates, pitted and chopped
2 small pears, cored and chopped

Blend the soy milk, dates and pears in a blender until smooth. Pour into glasses and serve. Makes 2 medium glasses.

Musky and full of promise, cardamom and honey infuse this shake with warmth.

spiced melon shake

1/4 teaspoon cardamom seeds
350 ml (12 fl oz) creamy soy milk
1/2 rockmelon (netted/US cantaloupe), peeled, seeded and chopped
1 tablespoon honey
2 tablespoons ground almonds
4 ice cubes

Lightly crush the cardamom seeds in a mortar and pestle or with the back of a knife. Blend the cardamom and soy milk in a blender for 30 seconds. Strain the soy milk and rinse any remaining seeds from the blender. Return the strained milk to the blender, add the rockmelon, honey, ground almonds and ice cubes and blend until smooth. Makes 2 medium glasses.

Light, juicy watermelon cuts through the creaminess of this indulgent blend. Making it all right. Right?

watermelon smoothie

600 g (1 lb 5 oz) watermelon, peeled and chopped
125 g (1/2 cup) yoghurt
250 ml (1 cup) milk
1 tablespoon caster (superfine) sugar
2 scoops vanilla ice cream

Blend the watermelon, yoghurt, milk and sugar in a blender until smooth. Add the ice cream and blend for a few seconds, or until frothy. Makes 4 small glasses.

Serve with a stack of buttermilk hotcakes for a truly impressive breakfast.

summer buttermilk smoothie

2 peaches
1/3 small rockmelon (netted/US cantaloupe), peeled, seeded and chopped
150 g (51/2 oz) strawberries, hulled
4 mint leaves
125 ml (1/2 cup) buttermilk
125 ml (1/2 cup) orange juice
1–2 tablespoons honey

Cut a cross in the base of the peaches. Put them in a heatproof bowl and cover with boiling water. Leave for 1–2 minutes, then remove with a slotted spoon and plunge into cold water. Remove the skin and stones, and slice the flesh. Blend the peaches, rockmelon, strawberries and mint in a blender until smooth. Add the buttermilk, orange juice and 1 tablespoon of the honey and blend to combine. Taste for sweetness and add more honey if needed. Makes 2 medium glasses.

No-one can be peachy keen all the time, so fake it in style.

peachy keen

2 large peaches, stones removed
and chopped
60 g (1/2 cup) raspberries
185 g (3/4 cup) low-fat peach and
mango yoghurt
185 ml (3/4 cup) apricot nectar
8 large ice cubes
peach wedges, to serve

Blend the peaches, raspberries, yoghurt, apricot nectar and ice cubes in a blender until smooth. Serve with the peach wedges. Makes 2 medium glasses.

Dried apricots are potent packages of betacarotene, antioxidants, iron and flavour. They're also cute as buttons and very delicious.

apricot whip

75 g (2¹/2 oz) dried apricots
125 g (¹/2 cup) apricot yoghurt
170 ml (²/3 cup) light coconut milk
310 ml (1¹/2 cups) milk
1 scoop vanilla ice cream
1 tablespoon honey
flaked coconut, toasted, to garnish

Soak the dried apricots in boiling water for 15 minutes, then drain and roughly chop. Blend the apricots, yoghurt, coconut milk, milk, ice cream and honey in a blender until smooth. Serve sprinkled with the flaked coconut. Makes 2 medium glasses.

Pop the blueberry bubbles for a tongue-tingling explosion.

mango smoothie with fresh berries

2 mangoes, peeled, stones removed
and chopped
125 ml (1/2 cup) milk
250 ml (1 cup) buttermilk
1 tablespoon caster (superfine) sugar
2 scoops mango gelato or sorbet
50 g (1/3 cup) blueberries

Blend the mango, milk, buttermilk, sugar and gelato in a blender until smooth. Serve garnished with the blueberries. Makes 4 small glasses.

Go low on fat but keep the full-on flavour with this mineral-rich revitalizer.

banana date smoothie

2 bananas, chopped
50 g (^{1}/2 cup) fresh dates, pitted and chopped
250 g (1 cup) low-fat natural yoghurt
125 ml (^{1}/2 cup) skim milk
8 ice cubes

Blend the banana, dates, yoghurt, milk and ice cubes in a blender until smooth. Makes 2 medium glasses.

Best consumed on a Sunday with the papers in one hand and some waffles in the other.

blue maple

200 g (1 cup) low-fat blueberry fromage frais
185 ml (3/4 cup) low-fat milk
1 tablespoon maple syrup
1/2 teaspoon ground cinnamon
300 g (10 1/2 oz) frozen blueberries

Blend the fromage frais, milk, maple syrup, cinnamon and 250 g (9 oz) of the frozen blueberries in a blender until smooth. Serve topped with the remaining blueberries. Makes 2 medium glasses.

One a berry, two a berry, three a berry, four.

berry yoghurt smoothie

250 g (9 oz) strawberries, hulled
125 g (4½ oz) frozen raspberries
250 g (1 cup) low-fat strawberry yoghurt
125 ml (½ cup) cranberry juice

Blend the strawberries, 85 g (²/₃ cup) of the frozen raspberries, the yoghurt and cranberry juice in a blender until smooth. Serve with a spoon, topped with the remaining raspberries. Makes 4 small glasses.

Not a roadside attraction, just an excellent way to start the day.

big bold banana

750 ml (3 cups) soy milk
125 g (4½ oz) silken tofu
4 very ripe bananas, chopped
1 tablespoon honey
1 tablespoon natural vanilla extract (essence)
1 tablespoon carob powder (see Note)

Blend the soy milk, tofu, banana, honey, vanilla and carob powder in a blender until smooth. Serve with long spoons. Makes 4 medium glasses.

Note: Carob powder is available from health-food stores.

Indulge a passion for bananas with this filling thick-shake.

banana passion

3 passionfruit, halved
1 large banana, chopped
60 g (1/4 cup) low-fat natural yoghurt
250 ml (1 cup) skim milk

Scoop out the passionfruit pulp and blend with the banana, yoghurt and milk in a blender in short bursts until smooth and the seeds are finely chopped. (Add more milk if it is too thick.) Don't blend for too long or it will become very bubbly and increase in volume. Makes 2 small glasses.

A smooth sweet treat that's berry berry nice.

smoothberry

150 g (5¹/2 oz) strawberries, hulled
60 g (2¹/4 oz) raspberries
200 g (7 oz) boysenberries
250 ml (1 cup) milk
3 scoops vanilla ice cream

Place the strawberries, raspberries, boysenberries, milk and ice cream in a blender until smooth. Chill. Pour into glasses and serve. Makes 4 large glasses.

Get to know your papayas: choose heavy, yellowy-orange ones with soft, fragrant flesh.

papaya and orange smoothie

1 papaya, peeled, seeded and chopped
1 orange, peeled and chopped
6–8 ice cubes
200 g (7 oz) natural yoghurt
1–2 tablespoons caster (superfine) sugar
ground nutmeg, to serve

Blend the papaya, orange and ice cubes in a blender until smooth. Add the yoghurt and blend to combine. Add the sugar, to taste. Serve sprinkled with nutmeg. Makes 2 medium glasses.

Note: This keeps well for 6 hours in the fridge. Peach- or apricot- flavoured yoghurt may be used for added flavour.

Once you get started you may not be able to stop, so make sure there's plenty to go round.

blueberry starter

200 g (7 oz) blueberries
250 g (1 cup) natural yoghurt
250 ml (1 cup) milk
1 tablespoon wheat germ
1–2 teaspoons honey, to taste

Blend the blueberries, yoghurt, milk, wheat germ and honey in a blender until smooth. Makes 2 medium glasses.

Note: Frozen blueberries are great for this recipe. There is no need to thaw them.

Strong, smooth and powerful — a real super hero!

peanut choc power smoothie

500 ml (2 cups) chocolate-flavoured soy milk
125 g (4^1/$_2$ oz) silken tofu
60 g (^{1}/$_4$ cup) peanut butter
2 bananas, chopped
2 tablespoons chocolate sauce
8 large ice cubes

Blend the soy milk, tofu, peanut butter, banana, chocolate sauce and ice cubes in a blender until smooth. Makes 4 small glasses.

Let the season guide your footsteps — choose whatever fresh berries are available.

mixed berry and lemonade fizz

100 g (3^1/$_2$ oz) strawberries, hulled
50 g (1^3/$_4$ oz) blueberries
750 ml (3 cups) lemonade
2 scoops lemon sorbet
extra berries, to garnish, optional

Blend the strawberries, blueberries, lemonade and lemon sorbet in a blender until well combined. Pour into glasses and garnish with extra berries, if desired. Makes 4 small glasses.

Passionfruit has a unique intensity but vanilla more than manages, adding a smoothness all its own.

passionfruit and vanilla ice cream smoothie

170 g (6 oz) can passionfruit pulp in syrup
140 ml (5 fl oz) can coconut milk
250 ml (1 cup) milk
25 g (1/4 cup) desiccated coconut
1/4 teaspoon natural vanilla extract (essence)
3 scoops vanilla ice cream

Blend half the passionfruit pulp, the coconut milk, milk, coconut, vanilla and ice cream in a blender until smooth and fluffy. Stir through the remaining passionfruit pulp. Makes 2 medium glasses.

Buy these summer fruits by the tray and develop a smoothie habit.

apricot tofu smoothie

4 apricots, stones removed
2 peaches, stones removed
250 ml (1 cup) apricot nectar
150 g (5½ oz) silken tofu

Blend the apricots, peaches, apricot nectar and tofu in a blender until smooth. Makes 2 medium glasses.

When too much strawberry isn't enough, satisfy your cravings with this.

summer strawberry smoothie

250 g (9 oz) strawberries, hulled
250 ml (1 cup) wildberry drinking yoghurt
4 scoops strawberry frozen yoghurt
1 tablespoon strawberry sauce
few drops natural vanilla extract (essence)
ice cubes, to serve

Blend the strawberries, yoghurt, frozen yoghurt, strawberry sauce and vanilla in a blender until smooth. Serve over ice. Makes 2 medium glasses.

Grind away with your mortar and pestle for a fresh and spicy blast.

spiced mango lassi

3 mangoes, peeled, stones removed
and chopped
250 g (1 cup) natural yoghurt
250 ml (1 cup) milk
1 teaspoon honey
1 teaspoon ground cinnamon
$1/2$ teaspoon ground cardamom

Blend the mango, yoghurt, milk, honey, cinnamon and cardamom in a blender until thick and smooth. Makes 2 small glasses.

Note: Lassis are popular drinks in India where they are served alongside curries — the yoghurt cools and cleanses the palate. They can also be made with buttermilk.

Comfort yourself with a little pink milk at bedtime.

long tall raspberry and blueberry

200 g (7 oz) raspberries
200 g (7 oz) blueberries
500 ml (2 cups) milk

Chill 2 tall glasses in the freezer for about 20 minutes. Blend the berries in a blender until smooth. Pour 60 ml ($1/4$ cup) of the berry purée into a jug and carefully swirl in a spiral pattern around the inside of the glasses. Return to the freezer. Add the milk to the blender with the remaining purée and blend until thick and creamy. Pour into the glasses and serve. Makes 2 tall glasses.

Note: Any berries are suitable for this drink. Depending on the sweetness of the berries, you may want to add a little honey.

Make peace with your sweet tooth and indulge in a standing banana split.

creamy rich banana and macadamia smoothie

2 very ripe bananas, slightly frozen
100 g (3½ oz) honey-roasted macadamias
2 tablespoons vanilla honey yoghurt
500 ml (2 cups) milk
2 tablespoons wheat germ
1 banana, extra, halved lengthways

Blend the frozen bananas, 60 g (2¼ oz) of the macadamias, the yoghurt, milk and wheat germ in a blender for several minutes until thick and creamy. Finely chop the remaining macadamias and put on a plate. Toss the banana halves in the nuts to coat. Stand a banana half in each glass and then pour in the smoothie. Makes 2 large glasses.

Note: The bananas need to be very ripe. To freeze bananas, peel and chop them, toss in lemon juice and freeze in an airtight container ready for use.

Go the whole hog and serve this colada in cocktail glasses with lychees on toothpicks. Add a splash of white rum if you fancy a cocktail.

pineapple and lychee creamy colada

1/3 pineapple, peeled and chopped
750 ml (3 cups) pineapple juice
500 g (1 lb 2 oz) canned lychees
2 tablespoons spearmint leaves
125 ml (1/2 cup) coconut cream
crushed ice

Blend the pineapple, pineapple juice, the undrained lychees and spearmint in a blender until smooth. Add the coconut cream and crushed ice and blend until thick and smooth. Makes 6 medium glasses.

Note: The lychee is one of China's most cherished fruits and has been so for over 2000 years. As its season is relatively short, we've used canned lychees for this recipe.

Let this mineral-rich smoothie work its magic on any wayward moods or blood sugar levels.

banana and berry vanilla smoothie

2 bananas, chopped
200 g (7 oz) mixed berries
3 tablespoons low-fat vanilla fromage frais or whipped yoghurt
500 ml (2 cups) skim milk
1 tablespoon oat bran

Blend the banana, berries, fromage frais, milk and oat bran in a blender for 2 minutes, or until thick and creamy. Makes 2 medium glasses.

Note: The smoothie will be thicker if you use frozen berries. You may need to add an extra 125 ml (1/2 cup) skim milk to thin it down.

Ascend to berry yoghurt heaven with a clear conscience.

strawberry lassi

250 g (9 oz) strawberries, hulled
300 g (10¹/₂ oz) strawberry soy yoghurt
2 tablespoons honey
4 ice cubes

Blend the strawberries, yoghurt, honey, ice cubes and 2¹/₂ tablespoons water in a blender until smooth. Makes 2 small glasses.

Don't throw away black, spotted bananas — their lush ripeness is the highlight of this smoothie.

carob peanut smoothie

400 ml (14 fl oz) carob- or chocolate-
flavoured soy milk
2 very ripe bananas, chopped
150 g (5^{1}/2 oz) silken tofu
2 tablespoons honey
1 tablespoon peanut butter

Blend the soy milk, banana, tofu, honey and peanut butter in a blender until smooth. Makes 2 medium glasses.

If the evening sea breeze swept you away, rest and repair the morning after.

tropical morning soy smoothie

2 mangoes, peeled, stones removed
and chopped
350 ml (12 fl oz) creamy soy milk
150 ml (5$^{1}/_{2}$ fl oz) pineapple juice
15 g ($^{1}/_{4}$ cup) chopped mint
6 ice cubes
mint sprigs, to garnish

Blend the mango, soy milk, pineapple juice, mint and ice cubes in a blender until smooth. Serve garnished with mint. Makes 2 large glasses.

Breakfast is the most important meal of the day but there is no reason why it shouldn't also be the yummiest.

maple banana breakfast

350 ml (12 fl oz) fresh or creamy soy milk
150 g (5½ oz) vanilla soy yoghurt
2 very ripe bananas, chopped
1 large yellow peach, stone removed
2 teaspoons lecithin meal
2 tablespoons maple syrup

Blend the soy milk, yoghurt, banana, peach, lecithin meal and maple syrup in a blender until smooth. Makes 2 medium glasses.

Keep mum happy and make this breakfast-in-a-glass part of your routine.

get up and go smoothie

¹/₂ mango, peeled, stone removed and chopped
60 g (¹/₄ cup) vanilla soy yoghurt
500 ml (2 cups) fat-free soy milk
2 tablespoons oat bran
2 tablespoons honey

Blend the mango, yoghurt, soy milk, oat bran and honey in a blender until smooth. Serve with spoons. Makes 4 small glasses.

Frozen berries make the grade in all well-stocked freezers.

fruitasia smoothie

2 bananas, chopped
6 strawberries, hulled
100 g (3¹/2 oz) frozen raspberries
2 passionfruit, halved
100 g (3¹/2 oz) low-fat natural yoghurt
250 ml (1 cup) apple juice
2 ice cubes

Blend the banana, strawberries, frozen raspberries, passionfruit pulp, yoghurt, apple juice and ice cubes in a blender until smooth. Makes 4 small glasses.

Fill a thermos for an emergency breakfast on the run that works.

wheaty starter

2 breakfast wheat biscuits
2 bananas, chopped
60 g (1/4 cup) vanilla soy yoghurt
500 ml (2 cups) fat-free soy milk

Blend the wheat biscuits, banana, yoghurt and soy milk in a blender until smooth. Makes 4 small glasses.

We could all do with one of these!

good start to the day

2 bananas, chopped
1 large mango, peeled, stone removed and chopped
500 ml (2 cups) skim milk
500 ml (2 cups) orange juice or pink grapefruit juice

Blend the banana, mango, milk and orange or pink grapefruit juice in a blender until smooth. Pour into a large jug and chill. Makes 4 small glasses.

teas + tonics

Recover in style with the ultimate tummy soother.

ginger, lemon and mint soother

2 cm (³/4 inch) piece ginger, thinly sliced
125 ml (¹/2 cup) lemon juice
2¹/2 tablespoons honey
1 tablespoon mint leaves
ice cubes, to serve

Put the ginger, lemon juice, honey, mint and 750 ml (3 cups) boiling water into a heatproof jug. Set aside to infuse for 2–3 hours, or until cold. Strain and chill. Stir to combine and serve over ice. Makes 4 small glasses.

Note: This drink is delicious served the next day as all the flavours will have had time to infuse together.

Subtly spiced, this tea is a perfect match for a light lunch and salad.

cardamom and orange tea

3 cardamom pods
250 ml (1 cup) orange juice
3 strips orange zest
2 tablespoons caster (superfine) sugar
ice cubes, to serve

Put the cardamom pods on a chopping board and crack them open by pressing with the side of a large knife. Put the cardamom, orange juice, orange zest, sugar and 500 ml (2 cups) water into a saucepan. Stir over medium heat for 10 minutes, or until the sugar has dissolved. Bring to the boil, then remove from the heat. Set aside to infuse for 2–3 hours, or until cold, then chill. Strain and serve over ice. Makes 2 medium glasses.

Steeping the fruit and spices deepens the flavour of this golden infusion.

cinnamon and apple tea infusion

1 cinnamon stick
4 golden delicious apples, cored and
roughly chopped
3–4 tablespoons soft brown sugar
ice cubes, to serve

Put the cinnamon stick, apple, brown sugar and 1 litre (4 cups) water into a saucepan. Bring to the boil, then reduce the heat and simmer for 10–15 minutes, or until the flavours have infused and the apple has softened. Remove from the heat and cool slightly, then chill. Strain and serve over lots of ice. Makes 2 medium glasses.

Darjeeling, darling, is the only tea in town.

orange and ginger tea cooler

1/2–1 tablespoon Darjeeling tea leaves
zest of 1 small orange, cut into long, thin strips
250 ml (1 cup) ginger beer
8 thin slices glacé ginger
2 tablespoons sugar
4–6 ice cubes
mint leaves, to garnish

Put the tea leaves, half the orange zest and 500 ml (2 cups) boiling water in a heatproof bowl. Cover and set aside to infuse for 5 minutes. Strain through a fine strainer into a jug. Stir through the ginger beer and chill for 6 hours, or preferably overnight. An hour before serving, stir through the glacé ginger, sugar and remaining orange zest. Stir to combine, pour into tall glasses, add 2–3 ice cubes per glass and garnish with mint leaves. Makes 2 medium glasses.

Fragrant lemon grass works as a tonic for your soul as well as your body.

citrus and lemon grass tea

3 stems lemon grass
2 slices lemon
3 teaspoons honey, or to taste
ice cubes, to serve
lemon slices, extra, to serve

Discard the first two tough outer layers of the lemon grass. Thinly slice the lemon grass and put into a heatproof jug with 625 ml (2^1/$_2$ cups) boiling water. Add the lemon slices and cover. Set aside to infuse and cool to room temperature. Strain, stir through the honey, and chill. Stir to combine and serve over ice with extra lemon slices. Makes 2 medium glasses.

Note: For maximum flavour, only use the bottom third of the lemon grass stems (the white part). Use the trimmed stems as a garnish.

If no-one is watching, pop the tea bags over your eyes while you wait for this refreshing brew to chill.

iced lemon and peppermint tea

2 peppermint tea bags
6 thick strips lemon zest
1 tablespoon sugar, or to taste
ice cubes, to serve
mint leaves, to garnish

Put the tea bags, lemon zest and 830 ml (3$\frac{1}{3}$ cups) boiling water into a heatproof jug. Set aside to infuse for 5 minutes. Squeeze out and discard the tea bags. Stir in the sugar and chill. Stir to combine and serve over ice, garnished with mint leaves. Makes 2 medium glasses.

Note: Alternatively, pour about 125 ml (1/2 cup) of the tea mixture into 8 holes of an ice-cube tray. Freeze and serve with the chilled tea.

This herbal hit will have you skipping all the way to work.

iced mint tea

4 peppermint tea bags
115 g (1/3 cup) honey
500 ml (2 cups) grapefruit juice
250 ml (1 cup) orange juice
mint sprigs, to garnish

Put the tea bags and 750 ml (3 cups) boiling water into a large heatproof jug. Set aside to infuse for 3 minutes. Discard the tea bags. Stir through the honey and set aside to cool. Stir through the grapefruit and orange juice, cover and chill. Stir to combine and serve garnished with mint sprigs. Makes 6 small glasses.

When you fancy an old-fashioned afternoon tea party, sip this on the porch and see who comes a knockin'.

american iced tea

4 Ceylon tea bags
2 tablespoons sugar
2 tablespoons lemon juice
375 ml (1¹/2 cups) dark grape juice
500 ml (2 cups) orange juice
375 ml (1¹/2 cups) dry ginger ale
ice cubes, to serve
lemon slices, to serve

Put the tea bags and 1 litre (4 cups) boiling water in a heatproof jug. Set aside to infuse for 3 minutes. Discard the tea bags. Stir through the sugar and set aside to cool. Stir through the lemon juice, grape juice and orange juice, and chill. Stir through the ginger ale and serve over ice with a slice of lemon. Makes 8 small glasses.

Smoky and seductive, this sophisticated tea makes storm clouds disappear.

earl grey summer tea

250 ml (1 cup) orange juice
2 teaspoons finely grated orange zest
1 tablespoon Earl Grey tea leaves
1 cinnamon stick
2 tablespoons sugar, or to taste
ice cubes, to serve
1 orange, thinly sliced into rounds
4 cinnamon sticks, extra, to garnish

Put the orange juice, orange zest, tea leaves, cinnamon stick and 750 ml (3 cups) water into a saucepan. Slowly bring to a simmer over gentle heat. Add the sugar and stir until the sugar has dissolved. Remove from the heat and set aside to cool. Strain the liquid into a jug and chill. Stir to combine and serve with lots of ice cubes, garnished with the orange slices and extra cinnamon sticks. Makes 4 small glasses.

Mint juleps are just the ticket when the in-laws visit, but try to stay off the bourbon.

mint julep

20 g (1 cup) mint leaves, roughly chopped
1 tablespoon sugar
1 tablespoon lemon juice
250 ml (1 cup) pineapple juice
250 ml (1 cup) dry ginger ale
ice cubes, to serve
mint leaves, to garnish

Roughly chop the mint leaves and put in a heatproof jug with the sugar. Using a wooden spoon, bruise the mint. Add the lemon juice, pineapple juice and 125 ml (1/2 cup) boiling water, and mix well. Cover with plastic wrap and set aside for 30 minutes. Strain, then chill. Just before serving, stir through the ginger ale and serve over ice, garnished with mint leaves. Makes 2 medium glasses.

Classy as a cordial, this syrup also makes a divine sorbet.

lime and lemon grass syrup

4 limes

3–4 stems lemon grass, bruised and cut into 10 cm (4 inch) lengths

5 cm (2 inch) piece ginger, chopped

145 g (2/3 cup) caster (superfine) sugar

Juice the limes in a citrus press. Put the lime juice, lemon grass, ginger, sugar and 2 litres (8 cups) water in a large saucepan. Stir over high heat until the sugar has dissolved. Bring to the boil and cook for 1 1/2 hours or until reduced to about 375 ml (1 1/2 cups). Set aside to cool, then strain into a very clean glass jar or bottle and seal. Makes 375 ml (1 1/2 cups).

Note: To serve, pour a little syrup into a glass with ice and top with soda water or lemonade. Use stems of lemon grass as swizzle sticks.

Nutritious and soothing for the stomach, homemade lemon barley water is the real thing.

lemon barley water

110 g (1/2 cup) pearl barley
3 lemons
115 g (1/2 cup) caster (superfine) sugar
crushed ice, to serve
lemon slices, to garnish

Wash the barley well and put in a saucepan. Using a sharp vegetable peeler, remove the zest from the lemons, avoiding the bitter white pith. Juice the lemons in a citrus press. Add the lemon zest and 1.75 litres (7 cups) water to the barley and bring to the boil. Simmer briskly for 30 minutes. Add the sugar and mix well to dissolve. Remove from the heat and set aside to cool. Strain the liquid into a jug and add the lemon juice. Serve over crushed ice, garnished with lemon slices. Makes 4 small glasses.

Running low on funds? Take a tip from childhood and set up a stall.

homemade lemonade

685 ml (2³/₄ cups) lemon juice
275 g (1¹/₄ cups) sugar
ice cubes, to serve
mint leaves, to garnish

Combine the lemon juice and sugar in a large bowl and stir until the sugar has dissolved. Pour into a large jug. Add 1.25 litres (5 cups) water, stir well and chill. Serve over ice, garnished with mint leaves. Makes 6 medium glasses.

This pink tonic is just the ticket for a lazy game of tennis with the chaps.

raspberry lemonade

300 g (10^1/$_2$ oz) raspberries
275 g (1^1/$_4$ cups) sugar
500 ml (2 cups) lemon juice
ice cubes, to serve
mint leaves, to garnish

Blend the raspberries and sugar in a blender until smooth. Push the mixture through a strong sieve and discard the seeds. Add the lemon juice, mix well and pour into a large jug. Stir through 1.5 litres (6 cups) water and chill. Serve over ice, garnished with mint leaves. Makes 6 medium glasses.

Create your own costume drama with this ladylike tonic.

lavender and rose lemonade

juice and zest of 2 lemons
15 g ($\frac{1}{2}$ oz) English lavender flowers,
stripped from their stems
110 g ($\frac{1}{2}$ cup) sugar
$\frac{1}{2}$ teaspoon rosewater
edible rose petals, to garnish, optional

Put the lemon zest, lavender flowers, sugar and 500 ml (2 cups) boiling water into a heatproof jug and mix well. Cover with plastic wrap and set aside for 15 minutes. Strain, then stir through the lemon juice, rosewater and enough cold water to make 1.5 litres (6 cups). Chill well. Stir to combine and serve garnished with fresh edible rose petals, if desired. Makes 6 small glasses.

Beat granny at her own game with this zesty lemon refresher — just make sure you save her a glass.

just-like-grandma-made lemonade

15 lemons
330 g (1¹/₂ cups) sugar
ice cubes, to serve
lemon balm leaves, to serve
lemon slices, to serve

Juice the lemons in a citrus press. Put the lemon juice and any pulp in a large non-metallic bowl. Add the sugar and 125 ml (¹/₂ cup) boiling water and stir until the sugar has dissolved. Add 1.5 litres (6 cups) water and stir well. Transfer to a large jug, add ice cubes and float the lemon balm leaves and lemon slices on top. Makes 6 small glasses.

Note: If you can get your hands on lemonade fruit, it's perfect for this recipe – you may need less sugar.

Sweet memories in a glass.

rosemary and apple infusion

12 apples, juiced and strained or 1 litre
(4 cups) bottled apple juice
1 rosemary sprig
55 g (1/4 cup) caster (superfine) sugar

Combine the apple juice, rosemary and sugar in a large saucepan over high heat and stir until the sugar has dissolved. Bring to the boil, then remove from the heat. Allow to infuse for at least 1 minute, depending on your preferred strength of rosemary flavour. Strain and serve either warm or well chilled. Makes 4 small glasses.

Flush away any irritations with this spicy, cleansing tonic.

spiced cranberry infusion

1 litre (4 cups) cranberry juice
80 g (1/3 cup) caster (superfine) sugar
5 cm (2 inch) piece ginger, sliced
3 strips orange zest
2 cinnamon sticks
small pinch ground cloves
orange slices, to garnish, optional

Put the cranberry juice, sugar, ginger, orange zest, cinnamon sticks and cloves into a large saucepan. Stir over high heat until the sugar has dissolved. Bring to the boil, then turn off the heat but leave on the hotplate to infuse for 15 minutes. Strain and serve warm, garnished with a slice of orange, if desired. Makes 4 small glasses.

Breathe deep and inhale the aromas — a dreamy break is on its way.

ginger and lemon calm

3 cm (1¼ inch) piece ginger, sliced
1 lemon, thinly sliced
1 chamomile tea bag
honey, to taste

Put the ginger, lemon and tea bag in the bottom of a plunger or heatproof bowl and pour in 1 litre (4 cups) boiling water. Set aside to infuse for 10 minutes before plunging or straining. Serve with honey. Makes 4 small glasses.

Steeping the orange zest releases the precious oils that engender a sense of wellbeing.

vanilla and apricot orange infusion

200 g (7 oz) dried apricots, chopped
1 vanilla bean, chopped
zest of 1 orange
55 g (¼ cup) caster (superfine) sugar
small pinch cloves, optional
ice cubes, to serve

Combine the apricots, vanilla bean, orange zest, sugar, cloves and 3 litres (12 cups) water in a large saucepan. Stir over high heat until the sugar has dissolved. Bring to the boil, then reduce the heat and simmer for 20 minutes. Set aside to cool. Strain and chill well. Stir to combine and serve over ice. Makes 6 medium glasses.

No-one can be sweet all the time — celebrate the sharper side of life.

apple and cranberry infusion

200 g (2²/3 cups) dried apple
170 g (1¹/2 cups) dried cranberries
zest of 1 lemon
55 g (¹/4 cup) caster (superfine) sugar
ice cubes, to serve
fresh apple slices, to garnish

Combine the dried apple, dried cranberries, lemon zest and sugar in a large saucepan and add 4 litres (16 cups) water. Stir over high heat until the sugar has dissolved. Bring to the boil, then reduce the heat and simmer for 35 minutes. Remove from the heat and allow to cool. Strain and chill well. Serve over ice with a thin slice of fresh apple. Makes 8 medium glasses.

Note: Serve the leftover strained fruit with ice cream or use it for a pie or pastry filling.

You know it's good for you but you never knew it could taste so damn good.

iced kiwi green tea

6 kiwifruit, peeled
1 lemon, thinly sliced
2 green tea bags
2 tablespoons caster (superfine) sugar
ice cubes, to serve
kiwifruit slices, to serve
lemon slices, to serve

Juice the kiwifruit through a juice extractor. Put the lemon slices, tea bags and 1.25 litres (5 cups) boiling water into a heatproof jug. Set aside to infuse for 5 minutes. Discard the tea bags. Add the kiwifruit juice and sugar and stir until the sugar has dissolved. Set aside to cool, then chill. Stir to combine and serve over ice, with a slice each of kiwifruit and lemon. Makes 4 medium glasses.

Sweet yet subtle, this is a brew to daydream over.

iced orange and strawberry tea

3 oranges, peeled
500 g (1 lb 2 oz) strawberries, hulled
2 orange pekoe tea bags
ice cubes, to serve
orange zest, to garnish

Juice the oranges and strawberries through a juice extractor. Put the tea bags and 1.25 litres (5 cups) boiling water in a heatproof jug. Set aside to infuse for 5 minutes. Discard the tea bags. Stir through the orange and strawberry juice. Chill well. Stir to combine and serve over ice with a twist of orange zest. Makes 4 medium glasses.

Get a taste of island living with this piquant infusion.

minty pineapple iced tea

1 pineapple, peeled and chopped or 500 ml (2 cups) pineapple juice
2 English breakfast tea bags
10 g ($1/2$ cup) mint leaves
ice cubes, to serve
mint sprigs, to garnish

Juice the pineapple through a juice extractor, then strain the juice. Put the tea bags, mint and 1.25 litres (5 cups) boiling water into a heatproof jug. Set aside to infuse for 5 minutes. Discard the tea bags and mint. Stir through the pineapple juice and chill. Stir to combine and serve over ice, garnished with mint sprigs. Makes 4 medium glasses.

Alive with intense flavours, this sweet syrup lifts fizzy water into the realm of the divine.

passionfruit syrup

6 panama or large passionfruit, halved
125 ml (1/2 cup) lemon juice
115 g (1/2 cup) caster (superfine) sugar

Scoop out the passionfruit pulp and combine with the lemon juice, sugar and 500 ml (2 cups) water in a saucepan over high heat. Stir until the sugar has dissolved. Bring to the boil, then reduce to a simmer and cook for 11/2 hours or until reduced by half and slightly syrupy. Allow to cool, then strain, pressing on the solids. Pour into a very clean glass jar or bottle and seal. Refrigerate for up to 2 weeks. Makes 375 ml (11/2 cups).

Note: Pour a little syrup into a glass with ice, top with soda water or lemonade and serve.

Pour over vanilla ice cream for a sumptuous dessert.

cherry syrup

1.5 kg (3 lb 5 oz) cherries, pitted
4 strips of lemon zest
juice of 1 lemon
230 g (1 cup) caster (superfine) sugar

Put the cherries, lemon zest and juice, sugar and 500 ml (2 cups) water in a large saucepan. Bring to the boil and cook for 30 minutes, occasionally pressing on the cherries with a potato masher to release their juice. Strain through a fine sieve, pressing on the solids. Strain into a very clean glass jar or bottle and seal. Refrigerate for up to 2 weeks. Makes 500 ml (2 cups).

Note: To serve, pour a little syrup into a glass and top with soda water and a twist of lime. Also delicious with coconut milk and a dash of chocolate syrup over lots of ice.

drink finder

The drink finder is arranged so that you can find a drink by looking under its two base fruit/vegetable ingredients, by which we mean the two most dominant fruits or vegetables used in the recipe. If a drink has more than two of these base ingredients in its title, it will be listed under each one mentioned.

The fruits and vegetables have been listed according to the following major groups: apple and pear, berries, citrus, ginger, grapes, herbs and spices, melons, stone fruits, tropical fruits and vegetables. Check the guide below to see which fruits and vegetables are in these categories. For example, if you are looking for a drink containing oranges and pineapple, you will find it under citrus and tropical fruits.

Apple and pear: apple, pear

Berries: blackberry, blueberry, cherry, cranberry, raspberry, strawberry

Citrus: grapefruit, lemon, lime, mandarin, orange

Ginger: ginger

Grapes: grapes

Herbs and spices: basil, cardamom, chilli, cinnamon, dill, lemon grass, mint, parsley, tamarind, vanilla

Melons: honeydew, papaya, rockmelon, watermelon

Stone fruits: apricots, nectarines, peaches, plums, prunes

Tropical fruits: avocado, banana, guava, kiwifruit, lychee, mango, passionfruit, pineapple

Vegetables: beetroot, cabbage, carrot, celery, cucumber, fennel, spinach, tomato, zucchini

APPLE AND PEAR

BERRIES

CITRUS

GINGER

GRAPES

HERBS AND SPICES

MELONS

Delicious
breakfasts

Delicious breakfasts

Love Food is an imprint of Parragon Books Ltd

Parragon
Queen Street House
4 Queen Street
Bath BA1 1HE

Cover and internal design by Mark Cavanagh
Introduction by Bridget Jones
Photography by Don Last
Additional photography by Gunter Beer
Home Economist Christine Last

ISBN 978-1-4054-9640-7
Printed in China

Notes for reader
• This book uses metric and imperial measurements. Follow the same units of
measurements throughout; do not mix imperial and metric.
• All spoon measurements are level: teaspoons are assumed to be 5 ml and
tablespoons are assumed to be 15 ml.
• Unless otherwise stated, milk is assumed to be low fat and eggs are medium. The
times given are an approximate guide only.
• Some recipes contain nuts. If you are allergic to nuts you should avoid using them
and any products containing nuts. Recipes using raw or very lightly cooked eggs
should be avoided by infants, the elderly, pregnant women, convalescents and anyone
suffering from illness.

Contents

Breakfasts

Early bird or night owl, no matter when you feel energetic, breakfast is important for vitality. It will awaken your mind, re-balance your body, and provide energy and rejuvenating nutrients to keep you ahead of the morning and on track all day.

By morning, the body has digested yesterday's meals. Many people feel grumpy and lacklustre because their blood glucose levels have fallen overnight. Food and liquid raise blood glucose and prevent dehydration. Get into the breakfast habit and zing into life – there are lots of options and no excuses for missing out!

Personal best every day
This is lifestyle eating and it has to be just right. Key features of the best everyday breakfasts are familiarity, personal favourites, and practicality – they have to be quick and easy. Single people, couples, busy parents, children and teenagers have different takes on breakfast

– weekends may bring room to manoeuvre but Monday to Friday has to run like clockwork! Everyone has to be fed, watered, and on the way, some older children can help feed themselves, and some adolescents need to be persuaded to eat (they *so* need to eat breakfast).

Food to keep going
The ideal combination is some fast-acting source of energy for a wide-awake buzz (a large glass of juice is great) backed up by slow-release foods that will provide fuel until the next meal. Generally, morning food is designed to get you going with minimum effort and maximum return – cereals, toast and marmalade, fruit and yogurt.

Carbohydrates are important, especially the type that break down slowly, releasing energy over a few hours. Those are the complex carbohydrates – starches rather than sugars. The glycaemic index is a scale that rates

the speed with which carbohydrates are broken down and absorbed compared to glucose. It gives values of 0–100 known as GI values. The higher the value, the quicker the food is absorbed (glucose has a value of 100). Eating slow-release foods (low GI value) helps to avoid the hunger pangs and lack of energy.

High-fibre foods that are not highly processed (and not high sugar) provide energy for a few hours. Bran cereals and porridge oats are low GI and tortilla wraps, croissants and wholemeal bread are medium GI (stoneground wholemeal bread is low GI). Apples, pears, grapefruit, oranges, grapes, berries and bananas that are not too ripe are all low GI. Combining slow-release foods with others that provide instant energy slows down the energy rush. Fats and proteins slow down the process. Poached eggs, tomatoes and mushrooms with toast, followed by fruit, is a good mix. Homemade muesli is excellent – oats, grains, nuts, dried fruit, with milk, provide a great mix of nutrients, with 'good'

fat and protein from nuts, minerals and vitamins, especially if served with berries, apple or mango.

All days: all sorts
Breakfast is wonderfully versatile – savoury or sweet, delicate or substantial, food can be formal or on the move.

It's good to eat a variety of breakfasts – cereals some days; eggs on toast followed by fruit; yogurt with fruit, nuts and seeds; or toasted waffles with banana, nuts and yogurt. When time is tight, a smoothie can be whizzed and drunk in seconds (or prepared ahead).

Time to indulge
On birthday weekends, bank holidays, when friends stay, for an anniversary or Christmas...indulgent breakfasts are superlative! Scrambled eggs with smoked salmon, a classic cooked breakfast, or what about sweet treats, such as pancakes or warm croissants with home-made jam?

Rise & Shine

serves 2

3 large ripe sweetie
grapefruit or ugli fruit

150ml/5 fl oz sparkling water

1 tbsp runny honey (optional)

some slices of lime or peeled
kiwi fruit

2 tbsp yogurt

wake up sweetie

Halve the sweetie grapefruit and the ugli fruit and squeeze into
two glasses.

Add water and honey if liked.

Serve with a slice or two of lime or kiwi, floated on the surface
and topped with a spoonful of yogurt.

serves 2

250 ml/9 fl oz carrot juice

4 tomatoes, skinned, deseeded and roughly chopped

1 tbsp lemon juice

25 g/1 oz fresh parsley

1 tbsp grated fresh root ginger

6 ice cubes

125 ml/4 fl oz water

chopped fresh parsley, to garnish

carrot & ginger energizer

Put the carrot juice, tomatoes and lemon juice into a food processor and process gently until combined.

Add the parsley to the food processor along with the ginger and ice cubes. Process until well combined, then pour in the water and process until smooth.

Pour the mixture into glasses and garnish with chopped fresh parsley. Serve at once.

serves 2

250 ml/9 fl oz carrot juice

250 ml/9 fl oz tomato juice

2 large red peppers, deseeded
and roughly chopped

1 tbsp lemon juice

freshly ground black pepper

carrot & red pepper booster

Pour the carrot juice and tomato juice into a food processor and process gently until combined.

Add the red peppers and lemon juice. Season with plenty of freshly ground black pepper and process until smooth.

Pour the mixture into tall glasses, add straws and serve.

serves 2

2 large ripe Williams or
similar juicy pears

juice of 4 medium oranges

4 cubes crystallized ginger

pear, orange & ginger reviver

Peel and quarter the pears, removing the cores. Put into a food processor with the orange juice and the crystallized ginger and process until smooth.

Pour into glasses and serve.

serves 2

1 wedge of watermelon,
weighing about 350 g/12 oz

ice cubes

1–2 fresh mint sprigs,
to garnish

watermelon refresher

Cut the rind off the watermelon. Chop the watermelon into
chunks, discarding any seeds.

Put the watermelon chunks into a food processor and process
until smooth.

Place ice cubes in two glasses. Pour the watermelon mixture
over the ice and serve garnished with the mint.

serves 2–3

125 g/4¹/₂ oz whole blanched almonds

600 ml/1 pint milk

2 ripe bananas, halved

1 tsp natural vanilla extract

ground cinnamon, for sprinkling

almond & banana smoothie

Put the almonds into a food processor and process until very finely chopped.

Add the milk, bananas and vanilla extract and blend until smooth and creamy. Pour into glasses and sprinkle with cinnamon.

serves 1

1 banana, sliced

85 g/3 oz fresh strawberries, hulled

150 g/5^1/$_2$ oz natural yogurt

banana & strawberry smoothie

Put the banana, strawberries and yogurt into a food processor or blender and process for a few seconds until smooth.

Pour into a glass and serve immediately.

serves 1

25 g/1 oz blueberries

85 g/3 oz raspberries, thawed
if frozen

1 tsp clear honey

200 ml/7 fl oz live or
bio yogurt

about 1 heaped tbsp
crushed ice

1 tbsp sesame seeds

berry smoothie

Put the blueberries into a food processor or blender and process
for 1 minute.

Add the raspberries, honey and yogurt and process for a further
minute.

Add the ice and sesame seeds and process again for a further
minute.

Pour into a tall glass and serve immediately.

serves 2

250 ml/9 fl oz orange juice

125 ml/4 fl oz natural yogurt

2 eggs

2 bananas, sliced and frozen

slice of fresh banana,
to garnish

breakfast smoothie

Pour the orange juice and yogurt into a food processor and process gently until combined.

Add the eggs and frozen bananas and process until smooth.

Pour the mixture into glasses and garnish the rims with a slice of fresh banana.

serves 2

2 ripe bananas

200 ml/7 fl oz crème fraîche

125 ml/4 fl oz milk

2 tbsp clear honey, plus extra
for drizzling

$1/2$ tsp vanilla essence

banana breakfast shake

Put the bananas, crème fraîche, milk, honey and vanilla essence into a food processor and process until smooth.

Pour into glasses and serve at once, drizzled with a little more honey.

Healthy Start

serves 4

115 g/4 oz ready-to-eat dried
peaches

85 g/3 oz ready-to-eat dried
apricots

55 g/2 oz ready-to-eat dried
pineapple chunks

55 g/2 oz ready-to-eat dried
mango slices

225 ml/8 fl oz unsweetened
clear apple juice

4 tbsp low-fat natural yogurt
(optional)

exotic dried fruit compote

Put the dried fruit into a small saucepan with the apple juice. Bring slowly to the boil, then reduce the heat to low, cover and simmer for 10 minutes.

Spoon into serving dishes and top each serving with a tablespoon of yogurt, if desired. Serve immediately.

serves 4

1 pink grapefruit

1 yellow grapefruit

3 oranges

citrus zing

Using a sharp knife, carefully cut away all the peel and pith from the grapefruit and oranges.

Working over a bowl to catch the juice, carefully cut the grapefruit and orange segments between the membranes to obtain skinless segments of fruit. Discard any pips. Add the segments to the bowl and gently mix together.

Cover and refrigerate until required or divide between 4 serving dishes and serve immediately.

serves 2

1 small charentais,
cantaloupe or galia melon

2 kiwi fruit

melon & kiwi fruit bowl

Cut the melon into quarters and remove and discard the seeds. Remove the melon flesh from the skin with a sharp knife and cut into chunks, or if you have a melon baller, scoop out as much of the melon flesh as possible and place in a bowl.

Peel the kiwi fruit and cut the flesh into slices. Add to the melon and gently mix together. Cover and refrigerate until required or divide between 2 serving dishes and serve immediately.

serves 4

3 tbsp clear honey

100 g/3¹/₂ oz mixed
unsalted nuts

8 tbsp Greek yogurt

200 g/7 oz fresh blueberries

greek yogurt with honey, nuts & blueberries

Heat the honey in a small saucepan over a medium heat, add the nuts and stir until they are well coated. Remove from the heat and leave to cool slightly.

Divide the yogurt between 4 serving bowls, then spoon over the nut mixture and blueberries.

serves 2

100 g/3^1/$_2$ oz jumbo oats

200 ml/7 fl oz apple juice

1 red apple, cored

1 tbsp lemon juice

25 g/1 oz toasted hazelnuts, chopped

^{1}/$_2$ tsp ground cinnamon

100 ml/3^1/$_2$ fl oz natural bio yogurt

2 tbsp runny honey (optional)

70 g/2^1/$_2$ oz fresh bilberries or blueberries

bilberry bircher muesli

Put the oats and apple juice in a bowl, cover with clingfilm and leave to soak in the refrigerator for an hour. You can do this the night before.

Grate or chop the apple and mix with the lemon juice to prevent discoloration.

Add the apple, hazelnuts and cinnamon onto the oat mixture and mix well.

Spoon the mixture into serving bowls and top with the yogurt. Drizzle over the honey, if using. Spoon the bilberries over the muesli and serve.

serves 4

for the granola

10 g/¼ oz rolled oats

5 g/⅛ oz sesame seeds

pinch of ground ginger

5 g/⅛ oz sunflower seeds

2 tsp freshly squeezed
orange juice

1 tsp runny honey

for the fruit cocktail

300 g/10½ oz deseeded
watermelon, cut into chunks

100 g/3½ oz fresh orange
segments

6 tbsp freshly squeezed
orange juice

1 tsp finely grated orange
zest

1 tsp peeled and finely sliced
root ginger

1 tsp runny honey

½ tsp arrowroot, blended
with a little cold water

watermelon, orange & ginger cocktail with granola

Preheat the oven to 180°C/350°F/Gas Mark 4.

To make the granola, put all the dry ingredients into a bowl, then add the orange juice and honey and mix thoroughly. Spread out on a non-stick baking tray and bake for 7–8 minutes. Remove from the oven, break up into pieces, then return to the oven for a further 7–8 minutes. Remove from the oven and break up again. Leave to cool on the baking sheet. The mixture will become crunchy when cool.

To make the fruit cocktail, put the watermelon and orange segments into a bowl. Put the orange juice and zest, ginger and honey into a small saucepan over a medium heat and bring to the boil. Gradually stir in the arrowroot mixture and cook, stirring constantly, until thickened.

Pour the mixture over the fruit and leave to cool. Cover and chill in the fridge.

Spoon the fruit into glasses and sprinkle over the granola.

serves 4

12 large portobello mushrooms, wiped over and stems removed

2 tbsp sunflower oil, plus extra for oiling

1 fennel bulb, stalks removed, finely chopped

100 g/3½ oz sun-dried tomatoes, finely chopped

2 garlic cloves, crushed

125 g/4½ oz grated fontina cheese

50 g/1¾ oz freshly grated Parmesan cheese

3 tbsp chopped fresh basil

salt and pepper

1 tbsp olive oil

fresh Parmesan cheese shavings

1 tbsp chopped fresh parsley

stuffed portobello mushrooms with shaved parmesan

Preheat the oven to 180°C/350°F/Gas Mark 4. Lightly oil a large ovenproof dish. Place 8 of the mushrooms, cup-side up, in the dish and chop the remaining 4 mushrooms finely.

Heat the sunflower oil in a non-stick frying pan, add the chopped mushrooms, fennel, sun-dried tomatoes and garlic and cook over a low heat until the vegetables are soft but not browned. Remove from the heat and leave to cool.

When cool, add the grated cheeses, basil and salt and pepper to taste. Mix well. Brush the mushrooms lightly with the olive oil and fill each cavity with a spoonful of the vegetable filling. Bake for 20–25 minutes, or until the mushrooms are tender and the filling is heated through.

Top with Parmesan shavings and parsley and serve immediately, allowing 2 mushrooms for each person.

serves 4

300 g/10¹/2 oz asparagus, trimmed

1 tbsp white wine vinegar

4 large eggs

85 g/3 oz Parmesan cheese

pepper

asparagus with poached eggs & parmesan

Bring 2 saucepans of water to the boil. Add the asparagus to one saucepan, return to a simmer and cook for 5 minutes, or until just tender.

Meanwhile, to poach the eggs, reduce the heat of the second saucepan to a simmer and add the vinegar. When the water is barely simmering, carefully break the eggs into the saucepan. Poach the eggs for 3 minutes, or until the whites are just set but the yolks are still soft.

Drain the asparagus and divide between 4 warmed plates. Top each plate of asparagus with an egg and shave over the cheese. Season to taste with pepper and serve immediately.

serves 4

225 g/8 oz broccoli

1 tbsp white wine vinegar

4 eggs

225 g/8 oz smoked salmon

for the dressing

150 ml/5 fl oz 8% fat fromage frais

1–1 1/2 tsp Dijon mustard

2 tsp snipped fresh chives

wholemeal or Granary bread, to serve

smoked salmon with broccoli & poached eggs

Divide the broccoli into spears then cook in boiling water for 5–6 minutes, or until tender. Drain and keep warm while you poach the eggs.

To poach the eggs, fill a saucepan three-quarters full with water and bring to a boil over low heat. Reduce the heat to a simmer and add the vinegar. When the water is barely simmering, carefully break the eggs into the saucepan. Poach the eggs for 3 minutes, or until the whites are just set but the yolks are still soft.

Meanwhile, divide the smoked salmon between four individual plates. Stir all the dressing ingredients together in a mixing jug until blended.

Place the broccoli spears on the plates, top each serving with a poached egg, spoon over a little dressing and serve with wholemeal or Granary bread.

serves 4

1 tbsp olive oil

3 shallots, finely chopped

500 g/1 lb 2 oz baby spinach
leaves

4 tbsp single cream

freshly grated nutmeg

pepper

4 large eggs

4 tbsp Parmesan cheese,
finely grated

baked eggs with spinach

Preheat the oven to 200°C/400°F/Gas Mark 6. Heat the oil in
a frying pan over a medium heat, add the shallots and cook,
stirring frequently, for 4–5 minutes, or until soft. Add the
spinach, cover and cook for 2–3 minutes, or until the spinach
has wilted. Remove the lid and cook until all the liquid has
evaporated.

Add the cream to the spinach and season to taste with nutmeg
and pepper. Spread the spinach mixture over the base of
4 shallow gratin dishes and make a well in the mixture with
the back of a spoon.

Crack an egg into each well and scatter over the cheese. Bake in
the preheated oven for 10–12 minutes, or until the eggs are set.
Serve at once.

The
Big Breakfast

serves 4

1 tbsp white wine vinegar

4 eggs

4 English muffins

4 slices good-quality ham

for the quick hollandaise sauce

3 egg yolks

200 g/7 oz butter

1 tbsp lemon juice

pepper

eggs benedict with quick hollandaise sauce

To poach the eggs, fill a pan three-quarters full with water and bring to a boil over low heat. Reduce the heat to a simmer and add the vinegar. When the water is barely simmering, carefully break the eggs into the pan. Poach the eggs for 3 minutes, or until the whites are just set but the yolks are still soft.

Meanwhile, to make the hollandaise sauce, place the egg yolks in a blender or food processor. Melt the butter in a small saucepan until bubbling. With the motor running, gradually add the hot butter to the blender in a steady stream until the sauce is thick and creamy. Add the lemon juice, and a little warm water if the sauce is too thick, then season to taste with pepper. Remove from the blender or food processor and keep warm.

Split the muffins and toast them on both sides. To serve, top each muffin with a slice of ham, a poached egg and a generous spoonful of hollandaise sauce.

serves 2

300 g/10½ oz button mushrooms

15 g/½ oz butter

1 tbsp vegetable oil

salt and pepper

1 small red chilli, deseeded and finely chopped

1 tbsp soured cream

2 tbsp chopped fresh parsley

1 tbsp chopped fresh rosemary

slices of ciabatta bread, toasted

extra-virgin olive oil

handful of rocket leaves

mushrooms with rosemary, chilli, soured cream & rocket

Wipe the mushrooms with a damp cloth and slice thinly.

Heat the butter and vegetable oil in a wide sauté pan and add the mushrooms, stirring until well coated. Season lightly with salt and pepper and add the chopped chilli. Cover and cook for 1–2 minutes, or until the mushrooms have softened, then stir in the soured cream. Sprinkle over the chopped parsley and rosemary.

Serve with slices of toasted ciabatta, drizzled lightly with olive oil, topped with a few rocket leaves.

serves 2

4 eggs

100 ml/3½ fl oz single cream

salt and pepper

2 tbsp snipped fresh chives,
plus 4 whole fresh chives
to garnish

25 g/1 oz butter

4 slices brioche loaf,
lightly toasted

chive scrambled eggs with brioche

Break the eggs into a medium bowl and whisk gently with the cream. Season to taste with salt and pepper and add the snipped chives.

Melt the butter in a non stick pan over medium heat, pour in the egg mixture, and cook, stirring gently with a wooden spoon, for 5–6 minutes, or until lightly set.

Place the toasted brioche slices in the centre of 2 plates and spoon over the scrambled eggs. Serve immediately, garnished with fresh chives.

makes 6 soufflés

55 g/2 oz butter, plus extra, melted, for greasing

40 g/1½ oz plain flour

150 ml/5 fl oz milk

250 g/9 oz ricotta cheese

4 egg yolks

2 tbsp finely chopped fresh parsley

2 tbsp finely chopped fresh thyme

1 tbsp finely chopped fresh rosemary

salt and pepper

6 egg whites

200 ml/7 fl oz single cream

6 tbsp grated Parmesan cheese

sautéed button mushrooms, to serve

cheese & herb soufflés with sautéed mushrooms

Preheat the oven to 180°C/350°F/Gas Mark 4. Brush six 9-cm/3½-inch soufflé dishes well with melted butter and set aside. Melt the butter in a medium saucepan, add the flour and cook for 30 seconds, stirring constantly. Whisk in the milk and continue whisking over a low heat until the mixture thickens. Cook for a further 30 seconds. Remove from the heat and beat in the ricotta. Add the egg yolks and herbs and season well with salt and pepper.

Beat the egg whites in a clean bowl until they form stiff peaks then gently fold them through the ricotta mixture. Spoon into the prepared dishes, filling them just to the top. Place in a baking dish and pour in enough boiling water to come halfway up the sides of the dishes. Bake for 15–20 minutes, or until the soufflés are well risen and browned. Remove from the oven, leave to cool for 10 minutes, then gently ease out of their moulds. Place in a lightly greased ovenproof dish and cover with clingfilm.

Increase the oven temperature to 200°C/400°F/Gas Mark 6. Remove the clingfilm and pour the cream evenly over the soufflés, sprinkle with Parmesan and return to the oven for a further 15 minutes. Serve immediately with sautéed mushrooms.

serves 4

8 eggs

90 ml/3 fl oz single cream

2 tbsp chopped fresh dill, plus extra

salt and pepper

100 g/3½ oz smoked salmon, cut into small pieces

25 g/1 oz butter

slices rustic bread, toasted

sprig of dill, to garnish

scrambled eggs with smoked salmon

Break the eggs into a large bowl and whisk together with the cream and dill. Season to taste with salt and pepper. Add the smoked salmon and mix to combine.

Melt the butter in a large non-stick frying pan and pour in the egg and smoked salmon mixture. Using a wooden spatula, gently scrape the egg away from the sides of the pan as it begins to set and swirl the pan slightly to allow the uncooked egg to fill the surface.

When the eggs are almost cooked but still creamy, remove from the heat and spoon onto the prepared toast. Serve immediately, garnished with a sprig of dill.

makes 6 parcels

150 g/5¹/₂ oz feta cheese, crumbled

250 g/9 oz ricotta cheese

150 g/5¹/₂ oz smoked salmon, diced

2 tbsp chopped fresh dill

2 tbsp snipped fresh chives

salt and pepper

12 sheets filo pastry

100 g/3¹/₂ oz butter, melted, plus extra for greasing

4 tbsp dried breadcrumbs

6 tsp fennel seeds

smoked salmon, feta & dill filo parcels

Preheat the oven to 180°C/350°F/Gas Mark 4. Lightly grease a baking tray. In a large bowl, combine the feta, ricotta, smoked salmon, dill and chives. Season to taste with pepper.

Lay out a sheet of pastry on your work surface and brush well with melted butter. Sprinkle over 2 teaspoons of the breadcrumbs and cover with a second sheet of pastry. Brush with butter and spread a large tablespoon of the salmon mixture on one end of the pastry. Roll the pastry up, folding in the sides, to enclose the salmon completely and create a neat parcel. Place on the prepared baking tray, brush the top of the parcel with butter and sprinkle over 1 teaspoon of the fennel seeds. Repeat with the remaining ingredients to make 6 parcels.

Bake the parcels for 25–30 minutes, or until the pastry is golden brown. Serve the parcels warm.

serves 2–4

115 g/4 oz cooked peeled prawns, thawed if frozen

4 spring onions, chopped

55 g/2 oz courgette, grated

4 eggs, separated

few dashes of Tabasco sauce, to taste

3 tbsp milk

salt and pepper

1 tbsp sunflower or olive oil

25 g/1 oz mature Cheddar cheese, grated

fluffy prawn omelette

Pat the prawns dry with kitchen paper, then mix with the spring onions and courgette in a bowl and reserve.

Using a fork, beat the egg yolks with the Tabasco, milk and salt and pepper to taste in a separate bowl.

Using an electric mixer or hand whisk, whisk the egg whites in a clean bowl until stiff peaks form. Gently stir the egg yolk mixture into the egg whites, taking care not to over-mix.

Heat the oil in a large, non-stick frying pan and when hot pour in the egg mixture. Cook over a low heat for 4–6 minutes, or until lightly set. Meanwhile, preheat the grill.

Spoon the prawn mixture on top of the eggs and sprinkle with the cheese. Cook under the preheated grill for 2–3 minutes, or until set and the top is golden brown. Cut into wedges and serve immediately.

makes 12 pastries

butter, for greasing

500 g/1 lb 2 oz prepared shortcrust pastry

plain flour, for rolling

2 tbsp wholegrain mustard

12 streaky bacon rashers, diced, cooked and drained well

12 small eggs

pepper

125 g/4$^{1}/_{2}$ oz grated Cheddar cheese

2 tbsp chopped fresh parsley

mini bacon & egg pastries with cheddar

Preheat the oven to 180°C/350°F/Gas Mark 4. Lightly grease a deep 12-cup muffin tin.

Roll the pastry out to a 5-mm/¼-inch thickness on a lightly floured work surface and cut out 12 circles approximately 13 cm/ 5 inches in diameter. Use to line the cups of the muffin tin, gently pleating the sides of the dough as you ease it into the moulds. Place ½ teaspoon of the mustard into the base of each pastry case and top with a little of the bacon.

Break an egg into a cup, spoon the yolk into the pastry case, then add enough of the white to fill the pastry case about two-thirds full. Do not overfill. Season to taste with pepper and sprinkle the grated cheese evenly over the tops of the pastries. Bake for 20–25 minutes, or until the egg is set and the cheese is golden brown.

Serve warm, sprinkled with chopped parsley.

serves 6

2 red peppers, halved and deseeded

2 small chorizo sausages, diced

1 tbsp olive oil

2 potatoes, peeled and diced

handful of fresh basil leaves, torn into pieces

6 large eggs, lightly beaten

6 tbsp grated Manchego cheese

salt and pepper

tortilla with roasted peppers & spicy chorizo

Preheat the oven to 200°C/400°F/Gas Mark 6. Place the red peppers on a lined baking tray and roast for 15 minutes, or until the skins are black. Remove from the oven and cover with a tea towel until cool. When cool, peel away the skins and dice the flesh.

Meanwhile, cook the diced chorizo in a 30-cm/12-inch non-stick frying pan until it is brown and the fat is rendered. Drain on kitchen paper. Wipe out the frying pan, then heat the oil and cook the diced potatoes for 5 minutes, or until soft and lightly browned. Return the chorizo to the pan with the potatoes and add the diced red peppers and torn basil leaves.

Mix the eggs and grated cheese together and season to taste with salt and pepper. Pour over the ingredients in the frying pan, using a wooden spoon to distribute the ingredients evenly. Leave to cook for a few minutes over a low heat until the egg has begun to set. To finish the tortilla, place the pan under a hot preheated grill to brown lightly.

Slide onto a serving plate and cut into wedges to serve.

serves 4

8 lean back bacon rashers

2 beef or 4 medium
tomatoes, halved

4 eggs

3 tbsp milk

salt and pepper

1 tbsp snipped fresh chives

1 tbsp unsalted butter

bacon & tomato scramble

Preheat the grill to high and cover the grill rack with foil.
Arrange the bacon on the foil and cook under the preheated grill
for 3–4 minutes on each side, or until crisp. About 3 minutes
before the end of cooking time, add the tomatoes, cut-side up,
and cook for the remainder of the cooking time.

Meanwhile, beat the eggs, milk and salt and pepper to taste in a
medium-size bowl, then stir in the chives.

Melt the butter in a non-stick saucepan over a medium heat,
pour in the egg mixture and cook, stirring gently with a wooden
spoon, for 5–6 minutes, or until lightly set.

Arrange the egg scramble with the cooked bacon and tomatoes
on warmed serving plates and serve immediately.

Sweet Treats

makes 12 waffles
to serve 4–6

175 g/6 oz plain flour

2 tsp baking powder

$^1/_2$ tsp salt

2 tsp caster sugar

2 eggs, separated

250 ml/9 fl oz milk

85 g/3 oz butter, melted

100 g/3$^1/_2$ oz butter,
cut into pieces

3 tbsp golden syrup

3 large ripe bananas, peeled
and thickly sliced

waffles with caramelized bananas

Mix the flour, baking powder, salt and sugar together in a bowl. Whisk the egg yolks, milk and melted butter together with a fork, then stir this mixture into the dry ingredients to make a smooth batter.

Using an electric mixer or hand whisk, whisk the egg whites in a clean bowl until stiff peaks form. Fold into the batter mixture. Spoon 2 large tablespoons of the batter into a preheated waffle maker and cook according to the manufacturer's instructions.

To make the caramelized bananas, melt the butter with the golden syrup in a saucepan over a low heat and stir until combined. Leave to simmer for a few minutes until the caramel thickens and darkens slightly. Add the bananas and mix gently to coat. Pour over the warm waffles and serve immediately.

makes 18 pancakes
to serve 4–6

200 g/7 oz self-raising flour

100 g/3½ oz caster sugar

1 tsp ground cinnamon

1 egg

200 ml/7 fl oz milk

2 apples, peeled and grated

1 tsp butter

for the maple strup

85 g/3 oz butter, softened

3 tbsp maple syrup

apple pancakes with maple syrup butter

Mix the flour, sugar and cinnamon together in a bowl and make a well in the centre. Beat the egg and the milk together and pour into the well. Using a wooden spoon, gently incorporate the dry ingredients into the liquid until well combined, then stir in the grated apple.

Melt 1 tsp butter in a large non-stick frying pan over a low heat until melted and bubbling. Add tablespoons of the pancake mixture to form 9-cm/3½-inch circles. Cook each pancake for about 1 minute, until it starts to bubble lightly on the top and looks set, then flip it over and cook the other side for 30 seconds, or until cooked through. The pancakes should be golden brown; if not, increase the heat a little. Remove from the pan and keep warm. Repeat the process until all of the pancake batter has been used up (it is not necessary to add extra butter).

To make the maple syrup butter, melt the remaining butter with the maple syrup in a saucepan over a low heat and stir until combined. To serve, place the pancakes on serving dishes and spoon over the flavoured butter. Serve warm.

makes 10–12

140 g/5 oz plain flour

2 tbsp caster sugar

2 tsp baking powder

1/2 tsp salt

225 ml/8 fl oz buttermilk

3 tbsp butter, melted

1 large egg

140 g/5 oz fresh blueberries,
plus extra to garnish

sunflower or corn oil,
for oiling

butter

warm maple syrup

blueberry pancakes

Preheat the oven to 140°C/275°F/Gas Mark 1. Sieve the flour, sugar, baking powder and salt together into a large bowl and make a well in the centre.

Beat the buttermilk, butter and egg together in a separate small bowl, then pour the mixture into the well in the dry ingredients. Beat the dry ingredients into the liquid, gradually drawing them in from the side, until a smooth batter is formed. Gently stir in the blueberries.

Heat a large frying pan over a medium-high heat until a splash of water dances on the surface. Using a pastry brush or crumpled piece of kitchen paper, oil the base of the frying pan.

Drop about 4 tablespoons of batter separately into the frying pan and spread each out into a 10-cm/4-inch round. Continue adding as many pancakes as will fit in your frying pan. Cook until small bubbles appear on the surface, then flip over with a spatula or palette knife and cook the pancakes on the other side for a further 1–2 minutes until the bases are golden brown.

Transfer the pancakes to a warmed plate and keep warm in the preheated oven while you cook the remaining batter, lightly oiling the frying pan as before. Make a stack of the pancakes with baking paper in between each pancake.

Serve stacks of pancakes with a knob of butter on top, warm maple syrup for pouring and garnished with blueberries.

makes 8–10

115 g/4 oz plain flour

25 g/1 oz cocoa powder

pinch of salt

1 egg

25 g/1 oz caster sugar

350 ml/12 fl oz milk

50 g/1³/4 oz butter

icing sugar, for dusting

ice cream or pouring cream, to serve

for the berry compote

150 g/5¹/2 oz fresh blackberries

150 g/5¹/2 oz fresh blueberries

225 g/8 oz fresh raspberries

55 g/2 oz caster sugar

juice of ¹/2 lemon

¹/2 tsp mixed spice (optional)

chocolate pancakes with berry compote

Preheat the oven to 140°C/275°F/Gas Mark 1. Sift the flour, cocoa powder and salt together into a large bowl and make a well in the centre.

Beat the egg, sugar and half the milk together in a separate bowl, then pour the mixture into the dry ingredients. Beat the dry ingredients into the liquid, gradually drawing them in from the side, until a smooth batter is formed. Gradually beat in the remaining milk. Pour the batter into a jug.

Heat an 18-cm/7-inch non-stick frying pan over a medium heat and add 1 teaspoon of the butter.

When the butter has melted, pour in enough batter just to cover the base, then swirl it round the pan while tilting it so that you have a thin, even layer. Cook for 30 seconds and then lift up the edge of the pancake to check if it is cooked. Loosen the pancake around the edge, then flip it over with a spatula or palette knife. Alternatively, toss the pancake by flipping the frying pan quickly with a flick of the wrist and catching it carefully. Cook on the other side until the base is golden brown.

Transfer the pancake to a warmed plate and keep warm in the preheated oven while you cook the remaining batter, adding the remaining butter to the frying pan as necessary. Make a stack of the pancakes with baking paper in between each pancake.

To make the compote, pick over the berries and put in a saucepan with the sugar, lemon juice and mixed spice, if using. Cook over a low heat until the sugar has dissolved and the berries are warmed through. Do not overcook.

Put a pancake on a warmed serving plate and spoon some of the compote onto the centre. Either roll or fold the pancake and dust with icing sugar. Repeat with the remaining pancakes. Serve with ice cream or pouring cream.

serves 4

4 eggs, plus 1 extra egg white

1/4 tsp ground cinnamon

1/4 tsp mixed spice

85 g/3 oz caster sugar

50 ml/2 fl oz freshly squeezed orange juice

300 g/10 1/2 oz mixed fresh seasonal berries, such as strawberries, raspberries and blueberries, picked over and hulled

4 slices thick white bread

1 tbsp butter, melted

fresh mint sprigs, to decorate

spiced french toast with seasonal berries

Preheat the oven to 220°C/425°F/Gas Mark 7. Put the eggs and egg white in a large, shallow bowl or dish and whisk together with a fork. Add the cinnamon and mixed spice and whisk until combined.

To prepare the berries, put the sugar and orange juice in a saucepan and bring to the boil over a low heat, stirring until the sugar has dissolved. Add the berries, remove from the heat and leave to cool for 10 minutes.

Meanwhile, soak the bread slices in the egg mixture for about 1 minute on each side. Brush a large baking sheet with the melted butter and place the bread slices on the sheet. Bake in the preheated oven for 5–7 minutes, or until lightly browned. Turn the slices over and bake for a further 2–3 minutes. Serve the berries spooned over the toast and decorated with mint sprigs.

serves 8

125 g/4¹/₂ oz butter, softened, plus extra for greasing

100 g/3¹/₂ oz caster sugar

55 g/2 oz soft brown sugar

3 eggs

1 tsp vanilla extract

3 large, ripe bananas

250 g/9 oz self-raising flour

1 tsp freshly grated nutmeg

1 tsp ground cinnamon

mascarpone cheese or natural yogurt, to serve

icing sugar, sifted, for dusting (optional)

for the strawberry compote

85 g/3 oz soft brown sugar

juice of 2 oranges

grated rind of 1 orange

1 cinnamon stick

400 g/14 oz fresh strawberries, hulled and thickly sliced

banana bread with strawberry compote & mascarpone

Preheat the oven to 180°C/350°F/Gas Mark 4. Grease a 23 x 11-cm/ 9 x 4¹/4-inch loaf tin and line the base with non-stick baking paper.

Put the butter and sugars in a bowl and beat together until light and fluffy. Mix in the eggs, one at a time, then mix in the vanilla extract. Peel the bananas and mash roughly with a fork. Stir gently into the batter mixture, then add the flour, nutmeg and cinnamon, stirring until just combined.

Pour the mixture into the prepared tin and bake in the preheated oven for 1¹/4 hours, or until a skewer inserted into the centre comes out clean. Leave in the tin for 5 minutes before turning out onto a wire rack to cool.

To make the compote, put the sugar, orange juice and rind and cinnamon stick in a saucepan and bring to the boil. Add the strawberries and return to the boil. Remove from the heat, pour into a clean heatproof bowl and leave to cool. Remove the cinnamon stick. Serve slices of the banana bread with a dollop of mascarpone cheese or yogurt and spoon over the warm or cold compote. Dust with sifted icing sugar if desired.

makes 8 rolls

350 g/12 oz self-raising flour

pinch of salt

2 tbsp caster sugar

1 tsp ground cinnamon

100 g/3¹/2 oz butter, melted, plus extra for greasing

2 egg yolks

200 ml/7 fl oz milk, plus extra for glazing

for the filling

1 tsp ground cinnamon

55 g/2 oz soft brown sugar

2 tbsp caster sugar

1 tbsp butter, melted

for the icing

125 g/4¹/2 oz icing sugar, sifted

2 tbsp cream cheese, softened

1 tbsp butter, softened

about 30 ml/1 fl oz boiling water

1 tsp vanilla essence

simple cinnamon rolls

Preheat the oven to 180°C/350°F/Gas Mark 4. Grease a 20-cm/8-inch round tin and line the base with baking paper.

Mix the flour, salt, caster sugar and cinnamon together in a large bowl. Whisk the butter, egg yolks and milk together and combine with the dry ingredients to make a soft dough. Turn out onto a large piece of greaseproof paper lightly sprinkled with flour, and roll out to a rectangle 30 x 25 cm/12 x 10 inches.

To make the filling, mix the ingredients together, spread evenly over the dough and roll up, Swiss-roll style, to form a log. Using a sharp knife, cut the dough into 8 even-sized slices and pack into the prepared tin. Brush gently with extra milk and bake for 30–35 minutes, or until golden brown. Remove from the oven and leave to cool for 5 minutes before removing from the tin.

Sift the icing sugar into a large bowl and make a well in the centre. Place the cream cheese and butter in the centre, pour over the water and stir to mix. Add extra boiling water, a few drops at a time, until the icing coats the back of a spoon. Stir in the vanilla essence. Drizzle over the rolls. Serve warm or cold.

makes 12 croissants

500 g/1 lb 2 oz strong white
bread flour, plus extra for
rolling

40 g/1^1/$_2$ oz caster sugar

1 tsp salt

2 tsp easy-blend dried yeast

300 ml/10 fl oz milk, heated
until just warm to the touch

300 g/10^1/$_2$ oz butter,
softened, plus extra
for greasing

1 egg, lightly beaten with
1 tbsp milk, for glazing

fresh croissants

Preheat the oven to 200°C/400°F/gas mark 6. Stir the dry
ingredients into a large bowl, make a well in the centre and
add the milk. Mix to a soft dough, adding more milk if too dry.
Knead on a lightly floured work surface for 5–10 minutes, or
until smooth and elastic. Leave to rise in a large greased bowl,
covered, in a warm place until doubled in size. Meanwhile,
flatten the butter with a rolling pin between 2 sheets of
greaseproof paper to form a rectangle about 5 mm/¼ inch
thick, then chill.

Knead the dough for 1 minute. Remove the butter from the
refrigerator and leave to soften slightly. Roll out the dough on
a well-floured work surface to 46 x 15 cm/18 x 6 inches. Place
the butter in the centre, folding up the sides and squeezing the
edges together gently. With the short end of the dough towards
you, fold the top third down towards the centre, then fold the
bottom third up. Rotate 90° clockwise so that the fold is to your
left and the top flap towards your right. Roll out to a rectangle
and fold again. If the butter feels soft, wrap the dough in
clingfilm and chill. Repeat the rolling process twice more.
Cut the dough in half. Roll out one half into a triangle 5 mm/
¼ inch thick (keep the other half refrigerated). Use a cardboard
triangular template, base 18 cm/7 inches and sides 20 cm/
8 inches, to cut out the croissants.

Brush the triangles lightly with the glaze. Roll into croissant
shapes, starting at the base and tucking the point underneath
to prevent unrolling while cooking. Brush again with the glaze.
Place on an ungreased baking tray and leave to double in size.
Bake for 15–20 minutes until golden brown.

makes 5 x 450-g/1-lb jars

1.6 kg/3 lb 8 oz fresh
strawberries

3 tbsp lemon juice

1.3 kg/3 lb granulated or
preserving sugar

strawberry jam

Preheat the oven to 180°C/350°F/Gas Mark 4. Sterilize five 450 g/
1 lb jam jars with screw-top lids.

Pick over the strawberries and hull – discarding any that are
overripe. Put the fruit in a large saucepan with the lemon juice
and heat over a low heat until some of the fruit juices begin to run.
Continue to simmer gently for 10–15 minutes until softened.

Add the sugar and stir until it has dissolved. Increase the heat and
boil rapidly for 2–3 minutes until setting point is reached. Test the
mixture with a sugar thermometer – it should read 105°C/221°F for
a good setting point. Alternatively, drop a teaspoonful of jam onto
a cold saucer, place it in the refrigerator to cool it, and then push
it with your finger. If it forms a wrinkled skin, it is ready. If not, boil
for a further minute and repeat.

Remove the saucepan from the heat and leave to cool for
15–20 minutes, to prevent the fruit rising in the jar. Skim if
necessary. Meanwhile, warm the jam jars in the preheated oven.
Remove and fill carefully with the jam, using a ladle and a jam
funnel. Top with waxed discs, waxed-side down, and screw on the
lids tightly. Wipe the jars clean and leave to cool. Label and date to
avoid confusion later.

Store in a cool, dry place. Once opened, it is advisable to keep the
jar in the refrigerator.

makes 10

280 g/10 oz self-raising
wholemeal flour

2 tsp baking powder

2 tbsp dark muscovado sugar

100 g/3$\frac{1}{2}$ oz ready-to-eat
dried apricots, finely chopped

1 banana, mashed with
1 tbsp orange juice

1 tsp finely grated
orange rind

300 ml/10 fl oz skimmed milk

1 egg, beaten

3 tbsp sunflower oil

2 tbsp rolled oats

fruit spread, honey or maple
syrup, to serve

fruity muffins

Preheat the oven to 200°C/400°F/Gas Mark 6. Place 10 paper muffin cases in a muffin tin. Sift the flour and baking powder into a mixing bowl, adding any husks that remain in the sieve. Stir in the sugar and chopped apricots.

Make a well in the centre and add the banana, orange rind, milk, beaten egg and oil. Mix together well to form a thick batter and divide among the muffin cases.

Sprinkle with a few rolled oats and bake in the oven for 25–30 minutes until well risen and firm to the touch or until a cocktail stick inserted into the centre comes out clean.

Remove the muffins from the oven and put them on a wire rack to cool slightly. Serve the muffins while still warm with a little fruit spread, honey or maple syrup.